Ambedkar on Population Policy

Contemporary Relevance

Nitin Raut

SHIPRA

Rs. 650, US$ 26

ISBN: 978-81-7541-715-1

2022, 3rd Edition
(*2nd Edition 2020, First Published 2014*)

Ambedkar on Population Policy: Contemporary Relevance

Published by:
SHIPRA PUBLICATIONS
LG 18-19, Pankaj Central Market,
I.P. Ext., Patparganj, Delhi 110092
Ph. 91 11 22235152/ 6152; 9650028065
info@shiprapublication.com
www.shiprapublication.com

Foreword

Dr. Babasaheb Ambedkar was the principal architect of India's democratic Constitution and builder of Modern India. He was an intellectual giant and his contribution in various fields is significant, substantial and spectacular. Many statesmen admired his erudition and scholarship. He was much ahead of his time. He was gifted with what George Bernard Shaw called 'normal eye sight' capable of seeing clearly in the distant future. People admired him as the "fountain head of wisdom and knowledge". He had enormous love for his country and her people coupled with enormous love for truth, justice and freedom of man.

In India, people are influenced by kinship or status as determined by caste, class, or creed. It appears difficult to disentangle a person's abilities and capacities as a worker from his caste, religion beliefs, social and geographical origin or other attributes that have little to do with his potential contribution to the society. Consequently, efficiency suffers because special abilities go unused. However, Babasaheb Ambedkar successfully rose above these parochial constraints and contributed enormously to the development of the society in post-independence India.

As a statesman, Dr. Ambedkar proved his mettle by introducing important Bills in the Bombay legislative Assembly, which was constituted after the elections held under the Government of India Act, 1935. The Bills were very much concerned with the burning issues of the society. He believed that 'Law' was a paramount agency of social change. He tabled the Bill to abolish the *Mahar, Mang Vetiah Watans*. He also moved the Bill to abolish the *Khoti* System.

Many people know him as a great statesman and lawmaker, but he was a great economist too. He was aware of the adverse consequences of uncontrolled population growth on the economy of emerging nations, like India. Therefore, he pioneered the introduction of the Family Planning Bill in the Bombay Legislative Assembly. This Bill was unique and radical. Dr. Ambedkar was ahead of his time and could visualise the colossal problem of population growth. He knew that this problem would be a menace for India in future. Dr. Ambedkar framed the Bill and it was moved by Mr. Rohan in the Bombay Legislative Assembly on his behalf and it was voted out.

However, Dr. Ambedkar continued his crusade of informing the younger generation of the problem of population explosion. He asked the young men to bear in mind that having many children was a social crime. He understood that if the Indians did not undertake measures to control the birth rate, it would accelerate population growth beyond control. Time and again, Dr. Ambedkar reiterated that prosperity, fame and superiority of the society could not be determined by its population.

Dr. Ambedkar's thoughts in the field of population study and his foresightedness proved to be true. At present, the population of India is about 122 crores. It is the second country in the world after China in terms of population. Almost 17 per cent population of the world is residing in our country. It is due to his foresight alone that one can judge the magnitude of this colossal problem haunting the society today.

The book *Ambedkar on Population Policy—Contemporary Relevance* by Dr. Nitin Raut is a commendable research work which presents the vision and views of Founder Father of our Constitution, Dr. Bhim Rao Ambedkar, on the problem of international importance, specially for India which are very much relevant even today to guide the policy makers in framing the population policy for the development of the nation. I am sure readers interested in the different aspects of population issue would find this volume useful.

Sukhadeo Thorat
Chairman
Indian Council of Social Science Research
New Delhi

Acknowledgements

When I was a student at the Department of Dr. Ambedkar Thought at Nagpur University I got to know about Dr. Ambedkar's views on the population problem and I decided to do research on that topic itself.

Dr. M.R Shamkuwar (former HoD, Dr Ambedkar Thought) encouraged me to do the research. But, unfortunately, he passed away and my work was incomplete. After that Dr Pradeep Aglave, the present HoD of Dr. Ambedkar Thought, encouraged me to continue the research work and I completed my research under his valuable guidance. I avail this great opportunity to express my heartfelt gratitude and indebtedness to Dr. Aglave for his sincere guidance, valuable suggestions, constant supervision, keen interest, encouragement, timely help and constructive criticism during the research period.

I owe my sincere thanks to Dr. M.L Kasare, former professor and HoD of Economics at Yeshwant Mahavidhalaya (Wardha) for his timely co-operation and valuable suggestions which helped me in enriching my research in all the aspects.

I am also thankful to Dr. Pratibha G. Taksande, librarian, for providing information about Census Reports for this research work.

I wish to express my deep sense of gratitude and respect to Dr. (Mrs.) Saroj Aglave, Dr. Kailash Thawre, Dr Manish Wankhede, Dr. Danraj Dahat, Mr. Pranay Dhawale, Sanghrash Aglave and Mr. V.S. Ramteke. Last but not the least, I will forever remain indebted to my wife, Mrs. Sumedha Raut.

Dr. Nitin Raut

Contents

1
Introduction

Dr. Babasaheb Ambedkar is known as the Principal Architect of the Constitution of India. He was also an eminent parliamentarian and a great emancipator of the downtrodden people.

Dr. Ambedkar was, in fact, a multifaceted personality and a versatile genius, as he was an erudite scholar, a reputed historian, a learned jurist, an outstanding statesman, an ardent champion of human rights, an eminent educationist, a pragmatic economist, an eloquent parliamentarian, a staunch believer in democracy and secularism and, above all, a humanist and a crusader for securing basic rights for the oppressed. Indeed, the epithets can go on endlessly. He left an indelible mark on the history of our country.[1] But, very few people recognise him as an economist and an authority to challenge the scholars of economics.

An important aspect of Dr. Ambedkar's versatile personality does not, however, seem to have attracted enough attention, especially in the light of his achievements in the field of equality, social justice and drafting of the Constitution that he was an eminent economist. This was also due to the fact that Dr. Ambedkar himself perhaps chose to underplay his role as a professional economist, as he was mostly preoccupied with vital issues of social justice and in the drafting of the Constitution.[2] Yet it would be grossly unfair to relegate his economic ideas to a secondary status.

Dr. Ambedkar extensively contributed to various economic issues covering concrete economic problems. Further, what is creditable is that though most of his economic writings were related to the pre-independence period, they reflect not only unique freshness, but also his deep insights into the problems. He approached and examined the economic issues with such foresight that his analysis and treatment of some of them is very much relevant even today.[3] His evidence before the Hilton Young Commission reflected his thought on the current Indian problems, such as landless labourers, small holdings, etc.

Dr. B.R. Ambedkar: A Strong Supporter of Birth Control

It is universally recognised that the general problems of the Indian economy are indeed serious. Mounting unemployment, rising number of poor people, growing social tensions, concentration of resources in the hands of a few, lack of proper distribution of income, negligible access of marginalised sections to public facilities, labour unrest, gender based discriminations, pitiable living conditions of urban slum dwellers, Scheduled Castes and Scheduled Tribes, agriculture industry mismatch, failures in the land reforms sector, faster population growth and lack of moral values are some of the issues of concern in our economy.[4] Dr. Babasaheb Ambedkar tried his best to raise these issues from time to time on every platform. Records show that Dr. Ambedkar, with his academic knowledge of subjects like economics, political science, constitution and law, contributed to the evolution of a developing philosophy and strategy of economics planning and development.[5]

Even after five decades of independence, we are facing basic economic problems, such as poverty, unemployment, slow rate of growth, slow rate of industrialisation, increasing population, unequal distribution of national income, low productivity in agriculture, etc. Dr. Ambedkar's life and career were fully dedicated to solving key socio-economic issues, which the nation is facing even today. The economic emancipation of the country lies in the thought of Dr. Ambedkar, enshrined in his speeches and writings on the constitution and constitutional developments.

Dr. Babasaheb Ambedkar put forth the economic thought when, for the first time in India, he rebelled against the *Jamindari* or *Khoti* system. He not only preached, but also activated it as a programme of the Independent Labour Party. He moved the Bills in the Legislative Assembly for the abolition of *Mahar Watan* System, *Khoti* System and measures for birth control.

Dr. Babasaheb Ambedkar founded the Independent Labour Party as a political party in 1936. He had defined the problem of over population in the election manifesto of his Independent Labour Party and said that over population was the major cause of poverty in India. It was mentioned in the aims of the party that "The party, however, believes that the fragmentation of the holdings and the consequent poverty of the agriculturists are mainly due to the pressure of population on land and unless the pressure is relived by draining off the excess population subsisting on land, fragmentation will continue, and the condition of the agriculturists will remain as poverty stricken as it is today."[6]

Immediately after Dr. Ambedkar's introduction of the 1935 Act of India, elections of the Assembly were held. Independent Labour party contested the election of the Bombay legislative Assembly. Dr. Ambedkar secured 14 out of 17 seats, which were contested. His success in the 1937 elections was outstanding and during the period of the Assembly, he used the forum of non-official resolution to invite attention of the party in power to some of the fundamental problems in the country in general and Bombay presidency in particular. He moved the resolution regarding the measures of birth control in the Bombay Legislative Assembly on 10 November 1938.[7]

Dr. Babasaheb Ambedkar was probably the only political leader in India, who had strongly advocated the cause of birth control. Gandhism was the most dominant political philosophy in those days in India and the thinking of a large number of Legislators was naturally profoundly influenced by the Gandhian approach to the problem. Gandhism opposed any artificial measures for birth control. Gandhi had faith only in the concept of self-control or abstinence. The ruling Congress party was committed to Gandhian philosophy and, therefore members of the Congress party in the Bombay Assembly were against the measures for birth control.[8] When the resolution was put to voting, 11 members who supported it were mainly from the Independent Labour party and all other 52 members opposed it. Thus, the resolution moved by Dr. Ambedkar was negated. It is very interesting and important thing that it was not the problem of over-population. That is why he mentioned the pressure of population on land and the stress given on birth control. After that, he moved a resolution regarding measures for birth control.

Then, leaders of the Congress party ignored the thought of Dr. Ambedkar regarding birth control. Now, everybody knows the problem of population growth. It is obviously clear that Dr. Ambedkar had a vision that if births are not controlled, it will create great problem of population growth. Political leaders, economists and social thinkers did not pay attention toward the thought of Dr. Ambedkar regarding measures or birth control. Hence, now India is facing a problem of population growth. It is a reality, which nobody can deny.

While studying the Ambedkar Thought, I realised that what Dr. Ambedkar said in 1936 and 1938, were absolutely true. But nobody thought seriously about the woes of population growth in those days except him. That is why I decided to conduct research on this subject. Therefore I selected my topic on 'Dr. B.R. Ambedkar's views on Birth control and its relevance in Modern India.' While studying this topic it is essential to know the nature of population problem.

Explosion of Population

For the last several decades the Western countries have been warning us about the 'population bomb', which is the rhetorical summing up the dangers inherent in explosive population growth in developing countries of Asia, Africa and Latin America.[9] Since 1950, there has been tremendous increase in population in most of the developing countries that was unprecedented and could not be anticipated earlier. This rapid population growth, which continued till 1980, has been mainly due to decline in death rates and continuing high birth rates. Though there was no significant decline in fertility in most of the countries in the less developed regions, progress has been made towards improvement in the mortality rate, particularly since World War II.[10] As a result, population has been growing significantly. Since then, there has been a serious problems of population explosion.

In March 1974, the International Labour Organisation issued a grave warning that unless the birth rate is cut tremendously and measures are quickly adopted to make the best use possible of all available resources now while there is still time, there will not be enough food in the world to sustain life for millions of people in the next century.[11]

The problems of population is almost everywhere in the world. Population explosion has made the sociologists worried about the future existence of man. It is one of the most fundamental of human problems.[12] It affects every aspect of man's life—individual, national and international. It affects the health, wealth and happiness of individuals and families; it affects the prosperity and progress of nations; it affects the international security and peace.

India is not alone in the bid to stem the population explosion. Almost every country is, in same measure, realising its evil consequence. The population of the entire world is rapidly increasing; in 1960, it was estimated as three billion and it grew up to be six billion and 55 millions in 2000. Population is increasing rapidly day-by-day. It is clear that the world population has doubled within 40 years.

The demographic explosion in developing countries, which form nearly two-thirds of the world's population, namely the people of Asia, Africa and Latin America, has caused a serious imbalance in world population growth. China is the most highly populated country in the world. In 2000, China's population was one billion and 277 million and India had one billion 13 million population. It means that India is the second in the world as far as high population growth rate is concerned. Today, world's population is six billion.

China and India together have two billion and 290 million population. Though China has more population, however, this country has succeeded in reducing the fertility rate. But India has not got more success to reduce fertility. It is projected that if the population increases at the current rate, India will take over China by the year 2045 to become the most populous country in the world. It is an alarm of danger for India. Dr. Babasaheb Ambedkar had a vision regarding the problem of the population growth. Therefore, he had given warning to India and he brought a resolution regarding measures for birth control.

It is necessary to know what the population had been in the B.C. era and how it's growing in the A.D. era. World's population growth is given in the Table 1.1.

There was only 20 million population in the 1st A.D. The growth rate of population was slow till 1650 A.D. The above table clearly indicates that the world population has more than doubled from 1650-1850 in a period of two centuries. After that, the world population doubled from 1850-1930, in a period of 80 years. Today, world population is more than six billion, so one can understand how the problem of population growth is becoming more serious.

Nature of Indian Population

India is a vast country. It is the second most populated and the seventh largest country in the world. Its area of 32,87,263 Sq. Km, extends from the snow-covered Himalayan heights to the tropical rain forests of the south. It appears that the first all India Census was organised in

Table 1.1: Growth of World Population (10,000 B.C. to 2000 A.D.)

Year	*Population*
10000 B.C.	1 Lakh to 10 Lakh
5000 B.C.	5 Lakh to 20 Lakh
1 A.D.	20 million
1300A.D.	400 million
1650A.D.	500 million
1850A.D.	1 billion
1930A.D.	2 billion
1960A.D.	3 billion
1975 A.D.	4 billion
1986A.D.	5 billion
2000 A.D.	6 billion

1872; however, Censuses have been conducted almost at regular intervals in this country. In 1872, the total population of India was 20.6 Crores. Looking back nearly four centuries, when population census on modern lines was non-existent, it is estimated that the population of India in the 16th century was around 10 crores (100 million).[13] Thompson and Lewis are of the opinion that between 1650-1800, conditions in India were not quite favourable to a considerable population growth because of political instability. They further add, "Civil stifle, with the consequent insecurity of life and property, the stagnation of agriculture, arbitrary taxation, and personal Government, have always had unfavourable effect on the death rate. Hence, it appears likely that India's population grew very slowly, if at all, during much of this period".[14]

Though the census has been organised since 1881, yet in actual practice, nobody seriously took population problem into consideration till 1930. It was only thereafter that the growing population became topic of discussion. The British rulers, then, made us believe that the main cause of India's poverty was its ever increasing population. Dr. Babasaheb Ambedkar also said that growing population is a main cause of poverty. It was in 1933 that, for the first time, it was publically declared by the Government that India's population was unwittingly[15] increasing.[16] In 1936 and 1938, two All India Population Conferences were organised to discuss population problems, and in these conferences, some of the scholars anticipated that in 1941, India's population will touch the 40 crore figure. When scholars were discussing the problems of population, political and social reformers were not aware of the population problem. But Dr. Ambedkar was thinking seriously about the same problem and he also moved a resolution regarding measures for birth control.

To focus the attention of the people towards population problems, Dr. Radha Kamal Mukharjee, Prof. Gian Chand, Dr. N.V. Sowani, Dr. P.C. Jain and Dr. S. Chandra Shekhar wrote many useful volumes. In these volumes, the problems of Indian population were analytically and carefully studied. In addition to these individuals, in the Indian Statistical Institute, Prof. P.C. Mahalnobis also made an attempt to collect population figures. The All India Health Institute, Calcutta (now Kolkata) soon after came in the field. At the Government level, however, attention was seriously paid in 1938 when a sub-committee of National Planning committee was asked to look into the problem. In 1943, the Healthcare committee set up by the Government looked into the problem. In 1944, the then Education, Health and Land Department set up the Population Data Committee under the Chairmanship of Y.M. Yeats with the purpose of advising the Government on the availability of data related to population growth in India.

In 1949, the Family Planning Association was founded in Bombay with the main object of making the people conscious about controlling population and family size. In 1951, with the aid of Rockefeller Foundation, the Gokhale Institute of Economics and Politics, Poona (now Pune), decided to have a separate department, which dealt with population and demographic problems.

In 1947, India became a free nation and decided to have planned economic development. The Planning Commission, therefore, decided to study the whole problem very seriously and thoroughly. A panel of health programme of the Planning Commission, in 1954 appointed a committee to report on the problems of population growth and family planning. This committee again set up two committees, namely: (a) the Population Planning committee, and (b) the Population Research and Programme committee. The main aim of both these committees was to find out as to why the population in India was very rapidly growing. In 1956, a family planning Board was set up by the Central Government and a Director of Family Planning was also appointed by the Government. In the same year, a sub-committee on demographic studies was set up by the Central Family Planning Board, under the Chairmanship of Prof. V.K.R.V. Rao. It was the committee, which proposed setting up of four Demographic Research centers, one each at an important location.

From 1872, when the Census began in India, fairly reliable population statistics were at hands. The following table shows the growth of population in India since 1891.

The Table 1.2 illustrates clearly that India's population was growing at a very slow rate up to 1921, but it started gathering momentum from that year onward. The year 1921 is, therefore, described by demographers as the year of 'big divide'. However, it is noted from the Table 1.2 that the population growth was even negative during the 1911-1921 decade. This is obviously due to the influenza epidemic in 1918, which took a heavy toll of 15 million lives. Similarly, no appreciable increase in the population is seen in the decade 1941-1951; the main reason being the partition of the country in 1947.

The large size of India's population is not the only problem. More serious is the rapid increase in the population.[17] This increase has started from 1921, and has been very large indeed since 1951. The growth has been so large that it has been described as a population explosion. Population growth till 1921 was small, even negligible. Whereas between 1901-1911, the population increased, there was actually a decline during 1911-1921. Overall, during 20 years between 1901 and 1921, the increase was in the order of about 129 lakhs. This works out to be a little more than six lakh or 0.27 per cent annually. This by any standard is a very slow growth.

When the absolute additions of population are rendered into the rates of growth, i.e., in percentage terms, the story, as expected, continues to be grim, but in a more meaningful way. Decadal growth

Table 1.2: Growth of Population in India (1891-2001)

Census Year	*Population (Crores)*	*Decennial Increase or Decrease (Crores)*	*Percentage Increase or Decrease During the Decade*
1891	23.59	–	–
1901	23.83	–	–
1911	25.20	+1.37	+5.75
1921	25.12	–0.08	–0.31
1931	27.89	+2.76	+11.00
1941	31.86	+3.97	+14.22
1951	36.10	+4.24	+13.31
1961	43.92	+7.81	+21.51
1971	54.82	+10.89	+24.80
1981	68.52	+13.70	+24.66
1991	84.39	+15.87	+23.85
2001	102.70	+18.14	+21.34

was more than 20 per cent before 1951 and more than 20 per cent thereafter. Overall, the growth rate since 1951 has remained within the range of 21.6 and 24.8 per cent. There is, no doubt, a slight decline in the rate during the seventies and the eighties. But this is of no significance. In the seventies, the decline of 0.14 percentage points can hardly be considered a decline. The decline in the eighties is, however, more at 1.16 percentage points. But when viewed as a development over a period of 10 years, it is at best a change of marginal importance. Despite these down movements, the population growth has become steady since 1951. But it is steady at a high level.

On an annual basis, the growth rate before 1951 has been lower than two per cent and over two per cent after it. There has been some acceleration in the rate during the sixties, and a slight deceleration thereafter in the seventies and eighties. However, these ups and downs are too little to have much impact on the population growth.[18] In the last decade of 1981-91, the growth rate (average exponential) works out to be 2.1 per cent per annum. This is higher than that of some countries with whom we should compare ourselves.

During the period 1980-1991 for which data are available, while India's population grew at 2.1 per cent, that of China's rose at 1.5 per cent. Even Shri Lanka's growth of population has been only 1.4 per cent during this period.[19] No doubt, some less developed countries including Pakistan (3.1%) experienced a higher growth rate in their population. But this is no consolation for a country like India, where with the existing enormous population, the additions to it at the present growth-rates are equally enormous.

However, in comparison to the developed countries, India's growth rate is very large indeed. The rate of population growth for the USA is 0.9 per cent; for Japan, it is 0.5 per cent and for the UK, it is 0.2 per cent.[20] If India's population continues to grow at the present rate, it will overtake China to occupy the first position as the most populous country. India's population is not only large in absolute size, but it is growing at an alarming pace. As such, the population, instead of being an asset, has in fact, become what is appropriately described as the population-explosion.

High Birth-Rate of India

Basically, population trends of any country are conditioned by the interaction of three determinants—fertility, mortality and migration.

Migration, however, as a factor determining population dynamics has lost the influence, which it had in the earlier centuries. Under Indian conditions too, migration as a determinant of population growth in the country is quite insignificant.[21] Hence, attention should be focused only on the remaining determinants, namely, the birth rate and the death rate. The data in respect to these two rates are given in Table 1.3.

The birth rate in India was 37.2 per thousand in 1981. It was about 31 per thousand in 1981. In 2001, India's birth-rate was 25.4 and death-rate was 8.4 only. Birth-rates are expressed per 1000 persons, and on an annual basis. For example, a birth-rate of 30 means that in a year 30 infants are born per 1000 persons living. Similarly, a death-rate of 15 means that in a year, 15 persons died per 1000 persons living.

Compared to birth-rate in many countries, India's birth rate is very high.[22] Not only is the birth-rate high, it has remained almost stable at a high level in very many years. In the 100 years or so since 1901, there has not been any marked decline. India's birth-rate fell from 49 to 37 in 1971-1980. There is, thus, a fall of only 12 till 1980 and 18 till 1991, which amounts to very little considering the long time-span of nearly a decade during which it has fallen.

Causes of High Birth-Rate

High birth rate in the country is not unexpected. This, in fact, is special feature of underdeveloped countries. Many ecnomic and non-

Table 1.3: Average Annual Birth-Rate and Death-Rate in India

Year	*Annual Birth-Rate (per 1000 Population)*	*Annual Death-Rate (per 1000 Population)*	*Natural Increase*
1901-10	49.2	42.6	6.6
1911-20	48.1	47.2	0.9
1921-30	46.4	36.3	10.1
1931-40	45.2	31.2	14.0
1941-50	39.9	27.4	12.5
1951-60	41.7	22.8	18.9
1961-70	41.2	19.0	22.0
1971-80	37.2	15.0	22.2
1981-86	33.2	12.2	21.0
1986-91	30.9	10.8	20.1
1991-2001	24.8	8.9	17.0

Source: Registrar General of India, Census Figures.

economic factors are responsible for this high birth-rate. Following are the major factors of high birth-rate.

1. Poverty: The growth of population and depletion of resources are often claimed to be the principal factors for the growing incidence of poverty in the world.[23] Again, it can be argued that this connection is not inevitable, but often reflects a failure or absence of government intervention, since it is possible to eradicate poverty; there is sufficient political will.

Poverty with such associated factors as poor diet, illiteracy, ill health, etc. keep the birth-rate high in under-developed countries. For example, poor people do not have any fixed standard of living to maintain, nor are there any special costs for maintaining and educating children. On the contrary, children at a very young age start helping their parents in work and, therefore, prove to be assets for the family. Again, because of the lack of savings, these children, when they grow up, provide security to their parents in old age. In this sense, they act like insurance for their parents.

Another aspect of poverty is the high infant mortality rate among the poor because of deficient diet, lack of medical facilities, unhealthy living conditions, etc. This means that the survival rate is very low. In order to ensure that some children do survive, poor people tend to have large number of children.

De Castro, in his book 'Geography of Hunger', has given another reason for the close relation between high fertility and poverty. According to him, there is an intensification of reproductive capacities in chronically starved people, which develops through a complex process, involving both physiological and psychological spheres, when certain organs, in particular the degenerating liver of the poor, are unable to induce to inactivity excess estrogens, which go into blood, resulting in a marked increase in the women's reproductive capacity. The psychological sphere includes the shrunken nutritional appetite. In this way poverty causes high birth-rate.

2. Religious and Social Attitudes: Religious and social attitudes are such that preference is given to large families. Among Hindus, for instance, it is accepted that without at least one son, it is not possible to get deliverance from the cycle of birth and rebirth.[24] According to Muslim religion, every person has the right to marry four times.

It is taken for granted that every young man and woman must marry. Unmarried people do not enjoy, in general, a respectable social status. As a result of such attitudes, we generally do not find unmarried men and woman, and married people without children.

Marriage is not only universal, but it takes place at an early age too. The average marriage age for females is about 16 years. If we remember that the puberty of Indian women in this hot climate starts at the age of 15, then it follows that women start fertilisation very soon after they enter the reproductive age, and it lasts till menopause at around the age of 45 or thereabout. This results in large number of births.

3. Illiteracy, Ignorance and Non-Availability of Birth-Control Devices: A proportion of population in general and women in particular are illiterate. In 1991, the literacy rate in general was only 52.1 per cent and among women it is still lower at 39.4 per cent. There is large ignorance about the biology of reproduction, and about the devices of birth-control among the masses. In the last few years, there has, however, been some improvement in this respect. Even now a substantial number of people have an adequate knowledge about the basics of family planning.

Many of those, who know about family planning, equate it with contraceptive or abortion, etc. Only a few regard it as equivalent to planning a family. Besides, the non-availability of birth-control devices freely has been an important contributory factor in keeping the birth-rate up. Those, who want family planning, find it difficult because the device is not readily at hand. In this sphere too, there has been some improvement, but this is far from adequate.

These factors have been so strong in their influence that the birth-rate has remained high for very many year. The message, thus, is clear that unless efforts are made in a big way, there is every likelihood that the birth-rate may continue to remain high.[25] Factors like the rise in per capita income, spread of literacy, etc. will no doubt help bring down the birth-rate. But as the experience of other countries shows, these actors take a long time to become effective. These factors affect attitudes of the people and naturally cannot show results in a short period. Further, the rise in per capita income in the country is so slow that it is not going to have any impact in the short period. The literacy rate also is rising at a very slow pace, and its influence too cannot be great in the short period. Hence, massive and sustained deliberate efforts are needed to produce any perceptible effect on the birth-rate in the immediate future.

Declining Death-Rate and Its Causes

The situation regarding death-rate is quite different. In the beginning of this century, the death-rate was as high as 43 per thousand. In underdeveloped countries such high rates are quite normal. Poverty, illiteracy, early marriage, lack of medical facilities etc. are the causes of many deaths. But what is noteworthy in the Indian context is that, despite the country being underdeveloped, the death-rate has been falling with the passage of time.

In the early stage, the decline was slow, but later on, especially after independence, the death rate fell rapidly. Death-rate was 42.69 per thousand annual during 1901-10, it come down to 31.2 during 1931-40, and was only 15 during 1971-80. It has further lowered to 10.8 in 1986-91 and again it came down to 8.4 during 1991-2001. Thus, in the last 100 years, the death-rate came down to about one-fourth of what it was in the beginning of the century. Following are the major causes of declining death-rate in India.[26]

1. Famines and Epidemics: In the earlier years, the high death was caused by several factors, of which the major ones were famines and epidemics. In those days, famines were almost a regular occurrence in some parts of the country. Due to lack of adequate transport facilities, food from one part of the country could not be made available to famine-stricken areas. As a result, large number of people died. Besides, epidemics like plague, cholera, malaria influenza, etc. used to take a heavy toll of human life in the country. During the 1901-10 decade, as many as 65 lakh people died of plague alone. Again, it has been estimated that during the short span of 1918-19, influenza took a toll of one and a half crore of people. Besides killing so many people, those who survived were weakened and rendered invalid, thereby shortening their life-span. Thus, it was largely the Malthusian checks, which operated.

Since 1921, however, there has been an improvement in this regard, especially after the attainment of independence. This is evident from the fact that death-rate after 1921 started falling; first at a slow rate and then at a rapid rate. Famines no longer cause the havoc they once did. After the terrible Bengal famine of 1943, the country has been practically free from famines. Floods and droughts even at present, cast their dark shadow on the country, but they are no longer as horrible as these used to be.

As a matter of fact, famines are now a matter of the past. The improvement in the situation has been caused by several factors, such as implementation of the schemes of agricultural development, streamlining of relief administration, extension of transport facilities, import of food grains, etc.

2. Medical and Health Facilities: The more important factors have, however, been the considerable improvements in the availability of medical facilities and public health services. These, together with the availability of facilities of pure drinking water and deter drainage, have enabled the country to control epidemics almost fully. The schemes for the extension of medical and public health services under the Five Year Plans have brought down the rate, reinforced by improved economic and social conditions in recent years. It needs to be remembered that autonomous factors affect more easily and in shorter time the death-rate than they do the birth-rate.

If follows that if necessary, public health services are available, and if adequate arrangements for medical facilities exist, the death-rate is bound to show sharper fall in a short period. In a number of underdeveloped countries, much before a reasonable advance on the front of economic development, the death-rate has shown a sizeable decline in response to health and medical facilities. Similar developments have taken place in India too.

3. High Natural Growth: If we take a look at both the birth-rate and the death-rate together, we would be able to explain the present rapid growth rate of population, in the beginning of this century, both the birth and the death-rates were high, with a small difference between both. Hence growth was slow. After some time the death-rate started falling rapidly, but there was no marked fall in the birth-rate. As a result, the difference between the birth-rate and death-rate continued to widen.

At present, the difference is about three times larger than it was at the beginning of the century. In the decade 1901-10, the birth rate exceeded death-rate by 6.6 per thousand. In the period, 1971-80, the excess of the birth-rate over the death-rate rose to 22.2 per thousand. For the periods 1981-86, 1986-91 and 1991-2001, the observed growth rates are large though somewhat lower at 21.2, 20.1 and 17.0, respectively.

Thus, the difference between the birth-rate and the death-rate explains why at present the population is rising so fast. Obviously, this rise in population has been caused by the fall in the death-rate, and not by a rise in the birth-rate. It follows that if the rate of population growth is to be reduced, efforts will have to be made to reduce the birth-rate.

Age-Specific Fertility Rate in India

With an increase in the mean age at marriage and the impact of family planning programmes, there is an overall decline in general fertility rate from 171 per thousand married women in 1988 to about 154 in 1993. It may also be noted that the decline is in all age groups, though the decline is sharper in the age groups 30-34 and above, as compared to the age group 15-19. There is a strong need to reduce fertility rates in the lower age groups, more especially, 15-19, 20-24 and 25-29, so that the general fertility ratio registers a sharps decline (*see* Table 1.4).

Fertility seems to have a strong correlation with the educational level of mother. Average number of children born to a woman, according to the census of 1991, was 4.3. This figure for illiterates was 4.4; for those, who were middle pass, but below graduation, it declined to 3.8; but for those with a graduate degree and above, it was only 2.3. Fertility in every category was higher in rural areas than in urban areas (*see* Table 1.5).

Table 1.4: Age-Specific Fertility Rates in India

Age Group (Year)	*1988*	*1993*	*Percentage Decline*
15-19	259.0	236.1	84.00
20-24	319.8	307.9	3.72
25-29	227.9	207.6	8.91
30-34	138.5	121.3	12.41
35-39	81.2	65.7	19.09
40-44	38.9	31.8	18.25
Total Fertility Rate	5.4	4.9	9.26
General Fertility Rate	170.7	153.7	9.26

Table 1.5: Number of Children Ever Born Per Woman in the Age Group 45-49 (1991)

Educational Level	*No. of Children Born*		
	Rural	*Urban*	*Total*
Illiterate	4.4	4.3	4.4
Literate below middle;	4.4	4.1	4.3
Middle but below matric;	3.9	3.7	3.8
Matric but below graduate and	3.1	2.9	3.0
Graduate and above	2.6	2.2	2.3
Total	**4.4**	**3.9**	**4.3**

Despite the above figures, as per India 2004, following States have very high fertility rate in India.

Uttar Pradesh - 16.2 per cent
Bihar - 8.1 per cent
Madhya Pradesh - 5.9 per cent
Rajasthan - 5.5 per cent

Therefore, we feel that much needs to be directed towards bringing the fertility rate of the above States to national limits.

Age Composition

The study of age composition is helpful in determining the proportion of the labour force in the total population. An estimate of the labour force in India is made in the 1981 Census report. The working age of the population is considered to be between 15-60. On this basis, the percentage distribution of India's population is shown in following Table 1.6.

These figures indicate that the proportion of child population in the 0-14 age group was 36.5 per cent in 1991. This figure is lower than the figures of earlier three decades. The principal reason for a higher child population in India is the high birth-rate. The recent decline in infant mortality has also added to our child population. The population of children only reflects a large proportion of unproductive consumers. To reduce the percentage of non-productive consumers, it is essential to bring down the birth rate. The decline in child population in 1991 is a reflection of the decline in overall birth rate in India.[27]

Table 1.6: Percentage Distribution of India's Population by Age Groups (1911-1991)

Year	*Age Group*		
	0-14	*15-60*	*60 and Above*
1911	38.8	60.2	1.0
1921	39.2	59.2	1.2
1931	38.3	60.2	1.5
1961	41.0	53.3	5.7
1971	41.4	53.4	5.2
1981	39.7	54.1	6.2
1991	36.5	57.1	6.4

Sources indicate that the proportion of child in 2001 Census further came down, while there is some increase in the proportion of the population of persons above 60 years of age. The reasons for both these factors are the same as indicated above.

Density of Population

Density of population means the number of persons per square kilometer. It is arrived at by dividing the number of persons by the total land area of a region/country.

In the last more than 80 years since 1921, the density of population has been a rising figure, and particularly since 1951, there has been a rapid rise. As per the 1991 Census, it is 274 as against 216 in 1981, 177 in 1971, 142 in 1961 and 117 in 1951. This, however, is the all India picture. At State level also, this has happened. But the change in the density has varied from State to State. In some States, it has increased much, in others not much, and in some other States, it is little indeed. Even within the States, there are differences in density in different regions. At present, we have 16.87 per cent of world's population while having only 2.4 per cent of world's land area (*see* Table 1.7).

Since the size of population has been rapidly rising, it is but inevitable, that given the geographical area of the country, there should be an increase in the density of population. However, equally and, perhaps more important, are the differences in the density of population of different States and of regions within States. The reasons for these differences are not far to seek.

India is primarily an agricultural country. Factors like climate, rainfall, irrigation facilities, etc. have a large bearing on the cultivation of land since these factors vary considerably in various States and regions. Huge differences are bound to exist in the density of population.[28] In north India, the land is very productive and the density is, therefore, very high. As against this, in Rajasthan because of sandy soil and deficiency of water, the density of population is low. So is the case of Jammu and Kashmir State with mountainous areas and of Madhya Pradesh with rocky lands, etc.

Another factor has been unequal development of industries in different States/regions. In some States, great strides have been made in industrial progress, resulting in the growth of industrial towns, cities and trading centers. All these centers attracted large population. As

Table 1.7: Density of Population in India

State/Union Territory	*Population in Millions*	*Density Per Sq. Km (1981)*	*Density Per Sq. Km (1991)*
India	843.9	216	267
Delhi	9.4	4,1947	6,319
Chandigarh	0.6	3,961	5,620
West Bengal	68.0	615	766
Kerala	29.0	655	747
Bihar	86.3	402	497
Uttar Pradesh	138.8	377	471
Tamil Nadu	55.6	372	428
Punjab	20.2	333	401
Haryana	16.3	292	369
Assam	22.3	230	284
Maharashtra	78.7	204	256
Andhra Pradesh	66.3	195	241
Karnataka	44.8	194	234
Gujarat	41.2	174	210
Orissa	31.5	169	202
Madhya Pradesh	66.1	118	149
Rajasthan	43.9	100	128
Himachal Pradesh	5.1	72	92
Jammu & Kashmir	7.7	59	76

against this, States/regions, which have not registered much industrial growth, have small density of population.

Besides, there are other factors that have influenced density at some places. These are the religious and historical importance of those places, the availability of educational facilities and the existence of administrative offices, etc.

Density and Economic Development: In this connection it needs to be noted that although economic factors influence the density of population, it is not a sure index of either poverty or prosperity of a country. The density of population of the USA is only 22, yet it is the most prosperous country. Brazil (density 12) and Australia (density 2) have the lowest densities, yet they are not as developed as the USA. At the other end is England with a very high density at 229 and yet it is one of the most advanced country. The same can be said about Japan with density at 221 and Netherlands with a high density at 329.[29] Thus, there is no direct relation between the density of population and the progress of a country. But one thing can be said about India with certainty that being an agricultural country, with some but not much industrial progress, the country is finding it difficult to bear the burden of the present high density of population. Since population is on the increase, the burden will become more unbearable unless there is (either/both) control over population growth or/and a faster rate of economic growth takes place.

Sex Composition

Sex composition shows the number of females per 1000 males. Information on this together with that on age-composition is very important for many thing like marriage-rate population growth, etc. In general, the death-rate among females, compared to that of males, is low because of biological reasons, enabling females to resist diseases more effectively than males.[30]

Thus, if the proportion of females is low, the death-rate will be affected favourably. Sex composition also influences the marriage rate and the number of children. Further, an unfavourable sex ratio, i.e., when the proportion of females is small, leads to the emergence of many moral and social evils (*see* Table 1.8).

As per the 2001 Census, there were 933 females for every one thousand males. In all, the total number of males is 53.01 crores (51.93%) and that of females is 49.06 crores (48.09%). Overtime, the number of females per thousand males has been falling till 1991 except for the decade 1971-81. In 1991, the number of females was 929 for every one thousand males. And it increased from 929 to 933 in 2001. The female-male ratio differs widely in different parts of the county. There is again a large difference in female-male ratio as between urban and rural areas, where it is lower in urban areas and in the rural areas, it is higher (*see* Table 1.9).

No commonly acceptable and satisfactory explanation can be given for the overall picture of lower numbers of females. However, a few reasons can be indicated. One is that girls in India are not as well looked after as boys. As a result, infant mortality among girls is high. Secondly, the burden of bearing children at an early age, the lesser use of birth control devices and the greater frequency of births at short intervals leads to the death of several women. Thirdly, it is doubtful whether at the time of Census, women are counted correctly. Because of the large illiteracy and social customs, which keep many women behind the curtain, quite a number of them go unreported. Four, as or larger female-male ratio in the rural areas, one of the possible reasons may be the fact that males go out of villages to work in cities, leaving their women folk behind.

Table 1.8: Sex Ratio in India's Population (1901 to 2001)

Year	No. of Females per 1000 Males
1901	972
1911	964
1921	955
1931	950
1941	945
1951	946
1961	941
1971	930
1981	934
1991	929
2001	933

Table 1.9: Sex Ratio in Different States of India (1991 Census)

State/U.T.	No. of Females per 1000 Males	State/U.T.	No. of Females per 1000 Males
Andhra Pradesh	972	Nagaland	890
Arunachal Pradesh	861	Orissa	972
Assam	925	Punjab	888
Bihar	912	Rajasthan	913
Goa	969	Sikkim	880
Gujarat	936	Tamil Nadu	972
Haryana	874	Tripura	946
Himachal Pradesh	996	Uttar Pradesh	882
Jammu & Kashmir	923	West Bengal	917
Karnataka	960	Andaman & Nicobar	820
Kerala	1040	Chandigarh	793
Madhya Pradesh	932	Dadra Nagar Haveli	953
Maharashtra	963	Daman & Diu	972
Manipur	961	Delhi	830
Meghalaya	947	Lakshadweep	944
Mizoram	924	Pondicherry	982
Total		**India**	**929**

Age Composition

Another aspect of population is its age-wise composition. It influences economic activities, as also the growth of population itself. The information on age composition is of significance for several reasons. One can know the size of the labour-force, i.e. those falling within the working age (normally 15-59 years). This number constituted 54 per cent of the population in 1981. Another significant segment is that of children, who fall in the age-group 0-14 years. This accounted for 39.5 per cent of the population.

This is quite a high proportion when juxtaposed with the proportion of children in the developed countries at 20-25 per cent. The cause of high percentage is the high birth-rate. A large fall in infant mortality rate from 183 per thousand in 1951 to 121 per thousand in 1981, has also contributed to this. The large proportion of children is indicative of the large number of unproductive consumers.

This means that the burden of dependents on the population is excessive. Old people above 60 years are about 6.5 per cent of the population. This small percentage is because of the low life-expectancy of the Indian population.

Life-Expectancy and Literacy Rate

Trends in the life-expectancy as also in the literacy rate are relevant in considering the improvement in the quality of life, as also in the productivity and family size in the country.[31]

Life-Expectancy: The number of year for which people of a country except to live at the time of birth is the average life-expectancy of that country. It depends mainly on the death-rate and the age at time of death. Thus, if the death-rate is high and/or death occurs at an early age, the life expectancy will be low. On the other hand if the death rate is low, life-expectancy will be high.[32]

Till recently, the life-expectancy in the country was very low. In the period 1901-10, it was only 23 years. In the next decade, it was estimated to be even lower at 20.2 years. It started rising, though slowly, after 1921. The rise became substantial from 1951. Life-expectancy was 41.3 years in 1961, 45.6 years in 1971 and 50.5 years in 1991.[33] The recent large increase in life-expectancy has been caused by a substantial fall in the death-rate and infant mortality rate. Even as such, it is much less than in some developed countries at over 77 years. Life expectancy in 2001 has increased compared to 1991 and it is not much as expected earlier.

Literacy Rate: The literacy rate has been on the increase, with a sharp step-up in the 1981-91 decade. As per 1991 Census, the literacy rate at 52.1 per cent marks a 8.5 percentages point rise over the previous rate of 1981 at 43.6 per cent. In 2001, the literacy rate was 65.38. It means literacy rate is increasing day by day (*see* Tables 1.10 and 1.11).

Table 1.10: Literacy Rate in India (1951 to 2001)

Years	Male	Female	Total Literacy
1951	27.16	8.86	18.33
1961	40.40	15.34	28.31
1971	45.95	21.97	34.45
1981	56.37	29.75	43.56
1991	63.86	39.42	52.11
2001	75.85	54.16	65.38

Table 1.11: Literacy Rate in Different States in India (1991 Census)

State/U.T.	Total Literacy	Literacy in Males	Literacy in Females
Andhra Pradesh	44.09	55.13	32.73
Arunachal Pradesh	41.59	51.45	29.69
Assam	52.89	61.87	43.03
Bihar	38.48	52.49	22.89
Goa	75.51	83.64	67.09
Gujarat	61.29	73.13	48.64
Haryana	55.85	69.10	40.47
Himachal Pradesh	63.86	75.36	52.13
Jammu & Kashmir	N.A	N.A	N.A
Karnataka	56.04	67.26	44.34
Kerala	89.81	93.62	86.17
Madhya Pradesh	44.20	58.42	28.85
Maharashtra	64.87	76.56	52.32
Manipur	59.89	71.63	47.60
Meghalaya	49.10	53.12	44.85
Mizoram	82.27	85.61	78.60
Nagaland	61.67	67.62	54.75
Orissa	49.09	63.09	34.68
Punjab	58.51	65.66	50.41
Rajasthan	38.55	54.99	20.44
Sikkim	56.94	65.74	46.69
Tamil Nadu	62.66	73.75	51.33
Tripura	60.44	70.58	49.65
Uttar Pradesh	41.60	55.73	25.31
West Bengal	57.70	67.81	46.56
Andaman & Nicobar Islands	73.02	78.99	65.46
Chandigarh	77.81	82.04	72.34
Dadra Nagar Haveli	40.71	53.56	26.98
Daman & Diu	71.20	82.66	59.40
Delhi	75.29	82.01	66.99
Lakshadweep	81.78	90.18	72.89
Pondicherry	74.74	83.68	65.63
Total	**52.21**	**64.13**	**39.29**

Literacy rate among females, both in rural and urban areas, is lower than that amongst males. As for States, there are great variations among them with States like Kerala showing highest literary rate in Indian States.

Despite UN uptrend in the literacy rate, it continues to be low and much below that achieved elsewhere, and as such, it is unsatisfactory. For example, the literacy rate is 100 per cent or near about in Sweden, the USA and England. No doubt, the literacy rate of India's population has gone up substantially since 1951. It is also possible to say that the literacy rate will continue to witness an uptrend in future.

However, it needs to be emphasised that the pace of increase in the past has been very slow. As such, greater efforts, including larger resources and a change in education policy favouring the schooling of the entire population till elementary education, have to be made, if the literacy is to be stepped up sharply.[34]

Though birth-rate of India is declining, however, death-rate is also declining rapidly. Therefore, India's population is increasing since 1921. That is why there is a serious problem of population growth in India. It is obvious that India has a serious problem of over-population since 1931. If Indian people could understand the vision of Dr. Babasaheb Ambedkar regarding population growth, there would not have been the problem of population growth in India.

Review of Empirical Studies

It is very necessary for this study to review some of the important empirical studies on population and the economy of Third World, with particular reference to India.

The problems arising out of the unprecedented growth of population in the developing countries are many and varied. Different studies touch upon the issues concerning the population problems, it nature and magnitude, and the possible solutions. Sidney Goldstein[35] examines the impact of migration on rural and urban populations, and concludes that there is a close inter-relation between rural and urban growth. As a result, efforts to solve the problems of the population sector exacerbate difficulties of other sectors in the developing countries.

Ravi Gulhati[36] examines the framework of India's population programmes and observes that half the couples in the reproductive age remain poor, and that the delivery system is not geared to their needs. That is why family planning programmes do not reach the most important target group. Therefore, he suggests the integration of family planning and rural development in India.

Stanley Johnson[37] discusses population growth in different parts of the world and presents some important implications of current demographic trends and their negative effects on migration, food supplies, housing, education, health and environment.

B.C. Mehta[38] analyses the relationship between population growth and various socio-economic factors in the Indian State of Rajasthan and finds that population growth has a negative impact on socio-economic development. He suggests a critical minimum effort to step up the rate of development in a situation of high population growth

P.S. Mohapatra[39] evaluates the national family planning programmes concerning the inter-relationships among ultimate programme objectives, the setting of activity targets, and the design of service statistics systems. He recommends programme managers, staff of programme evaluation units, and representatives of donor agencies for measuring effectiveness of the national family planning programmes.

B. Mondot and M. Jacqueline[40] examine the relationship between fertility, malnutrition and child mortality in African countries for devising a feeding policy for infants and young children, which would lead to the formulation of a consistent demographic policy.

V.P. Pethe[41] emphasises the need for voluntary family planning policy, which is based on democratic norms, social justice, and social transformation. Discussing the compulsory family planning policy in the less developed countries (particularly India), he states that compulsion in family planning is based on the neo-Malthusian approach, which contains errors and distortions. According to him, population problems are an integral aspect of the social conditions and, as such, they should be solved on the basis of social norms and traditions. He objects to the use of physical force in attaining the family planning targets, as was practiced in India during the National Emergency.

The United Nations[42] reviews the current and prospective population trends in Bangladesh with special reference to various social-economic factors, such as economic activity of population, health needs, housing needs, food supply and nutrition maintenance of law and order, and status of women. The United Nations[43] examines the problems and issues in measuring the impact of social and economic factors on fertility in the context of declining fertility. It[44] also examines the past, current, and prospective population trends in Nepal covering human and community needs such as health services, housing, education, employment, and family planning in terms of population size, growth rate, age composition, marital status, status of women and family size.

A. Adepoju[45] explores the recant economic demographic situation in selected African countries and examines the population problems in relation to development. A. Cigno[46] states that the assumption of a constant rate of population growth is implausible in an economy constrained by the function of consumption and capital per capita.

N.R. Crook[47] tried to relate population control with welfare and concludes that an economic evaluation of population limitation may not be possible for a country from the standpoint of social efficiency. Nick Eberstadt[48] studied the recent decline in fertility in the Third World and concludes that a decline in fertility does not necessarily mean an improvement in the standard of living and in the prospects for development.

D.R. Gwatkin[49] examines the mortality trends in the Third World and concludes that mortality trends have become more fragile and uncertain. Besides, the programmes for health improvement are capable of reducing notably or halting altogether the mortality trends. Pravin Visaria[50] reviews the Indian population policy and concludes that persuasion through monetary compensation as well as individual and group incentive is the best policy against compulsory sterilisation.

F.C. Alvarez[51] argues that the developing nations remain essentially colonised and dependent entities of the industrialised world. But, he concludes that the future world will be less unjust and better able to care for its own. V.V. Bhatt[52] discusses the dynamics of the social-economic system in terms of the cumulative and cyclical changes in economic institutions, ideologies, and technology. Further, he stresses the importance of upgrading traditional technology and also adaption of modern technology to given situations.

H. Chenery and M. Syrquin[53] examine principal changes in the economic structure, such as resource mobilisation and allocation, which are needed to sustain further growth of the economy. They conclude that rural-urban migration and lowering of the birth and death rates influence the demand for and supply of labour.

Brian May[54] assesses social conditions, politics, economics and cultural barriers in the Third World with particular reference to India, Iran and Nigeria and contends that there is chronic social and economic stagnation in these countries. Ignacio Sachs[55] proposes a general development theory to bridge the gap between European theory and Third World practice so that development strategies in the Third World become based on labour-intensive technologies. B.L. C. Johnson[56] reviews the development of India in the post-Independence era in relation to the environment and use of resources. Furthermore, despite contradictory evidence, he forecasts an optimistic view of the future of Indian development.

Ester Boserup[57] examines the inter-relationship between demographic and technological changes. By taking a cross-country comparison of recent data, she argues that demographic factors play a major role in inventions. According to her, population density determines whether certain technologies are economically viable or not. Lester Brown[58] examines the effects of rapid population growth on economic growth, the supply of food resources, environment and energy resources, and concludes that population growth has a depressing effect on the above factors. Finally, he proposes a strategy for stabilising world population growth.

According to J. Cairncross[59], there are close links between population and agricultural development in the developed countries, and the former has a positive impact on the latter. R.H. Cassen[60] examines India's contemporary economic and social problems from the point of view of population. According to him, population growth has contributed to the lack of material progress for the bulk of the population. His major findings are that India's population growth rate is past its minimum, the key development problem is the utilisation of labour at the village level, and the process of change required to alleviate poverty should confirm to the Indian socio-economic conditions.

S.H. Cochrane[61] examines the reasons for rapid fertility decline in Thailand, its regional differences and socio-economic consequences. He concludes that there is strong relationship between family planning programme inputs and contraceptive use. R.R. Faruquee[62] studies the factors inducing fertility decline and concludes that while family planning plays an important role, socio-economic development emerges as the most important factor in reducing fertility.

J.E. Kocher,[63] conducting case studies of India, China, Costa Rica and the U.S.A. examine the impact of rural development on demographic factors. His conclusion is that the greater the extent to which the rural population participates in the development process, the earlier and more rapid the reduction in fertility and overall population growth rate.

Research Methodology, Hypothesis, Aims and Objectives

According to Karl Pearson, "There is no shortcut to truths, or way to gain knowledge of universe except through the gateway of scientific method."[64] We can say that there is no research without research methodology. While conducting research, it is important to select the research methodology according to the research-subject, hence, research methodology is very important in any research. Present study is mainly based on secondary data. Therefore, the researcher has collected data regarding this study through secondary sources, i.e., books, periodicals planning commission reports, Census report, etc. For this study, the researcher has used the descriptive research design.

The study evaluates Dr. B.R. Ambedkar's views on birth control relating to present condition of Indian population. To what extent Dr. Ambedkar's view is relevant to the country; why India failed to maintain control on population growth; to what extent India is facing problem; and how it would be controlled; and to what extent the view of Dr. B.R. Ambedkar on birth control is true. All these questions have been discussed in this research work. The researcher hopes that this valuable work would be useful for formulating population policy for India. The impact of high rate of population on socio-economic aspects of the country has been focused in this study. Why Government failed to accept the view of Dr. B.R. Ambedkar? Why other members opposed the resolution regarding birth control? All related question are answered in this research work.

Following are the hypotheses of this study:

1. High growth rate of population affects the social, economic and educational progress of the country.
2. Increasing population is a hurdle in the way of development of the country.
3. Many economic, social and others problems emerge due to increasing population.

4. Dr. B.R. Ambedkar's view regarding birth control is relevant in the twenty first century.

The following are the aims and objectives of the study:

1. To scientifically study Dr. B.R. Ambedkar's view on birth control.
2. To study the effects of excessive growth of population on socio-economic aspects.
3. To study to what extent Dr. B.R. Ambedkar's view is relevant in the twenty-first century.
4. To suggest and find out other major suggestions to control population growth in general.

ENDNOTES

1. Abraham, P. (2002), *Ambedkar's Contribution for Economic Planning and Development: Its Relevance* and Kanishka Publishers, Distributors, New Delhi, p. 1.
2. *Ibid*, p. 8.
3. *Ibid*, p. 8.
4. *Ibid*, p. 8-9.
5. Gadekar, D. R., *Socio-Economic Thoughts of Dr. B. R. Ambedkar*, Lucknow.
6. *Dr. Babasaheb Ambedkar Writing and Speeches*, Vol. 17 Part Two, Dr. Ambedkar Source Material Publication Committee, Higher Education Development, Government of Maharashrta, Mumbai, 2003 p. 416.
7. *Bombay Legislative Debates*, Vol. 4 (Part-57) 10th November, 1938, pp. 4024-4038.
8. Mangudar, M. P. (1976), *Dr. Ambedkar and Family Planning, Pune*, p. 2.
9. Sinha, P. N., (2000), *Population Education and Family Planning*, Authors Press, Delhi, p. 239.
10. Malankar, C. R. (1997), *Populating Growth in Developing Countries, 1951-2025 in Demographic Transition: The Third World Scenario* (Edited) Aijazuddin, Ahmad; Daniel Noin and H. N. Sharma, Rawat Publications, Jaipur, p. 34.
11. Bahadur, K. P. (1977), *Population Crisis in India*, National Publishing House, New Delhi, p. 153.
12. Sharma, Yogendra K. (2005), *Population Education: Concepts, Principles and Approaches*, Kanishka Publishers, Distributors, New Delhi, p. 3.
13. Ogle, S. L. (1969), *The Tragedy of Too Many*, Academic Books Ltd.

14. Thompson, W. S. and D. T. Lewis, *Population Problems,* Tata McGraw Hill Publishing Co. 5th Edition.
15. Agrawala, S. N. (1967), *Population*, National Book Trust.
16. Raj, Hans (1993), *Population Studies*, Surjeet Publications, Delhi, (Part-III), p. I.
17. Sharma, Yogendra K., *op. cit*, p. 84.
18. *Ibid.*, p. 85.
19. *Ibid.*, p. 85.
20. *Ibid.*, p. 85.
21. Raj, Hans, *op. cit.* p. 24.
22. Sharma, Yogendra K., *op. cit.* p. 86.
23. Shroff, Meera (2004), *Population and Sustainable Development*, Adhyan Publishers and Distributors, Delhi, p. 12.
24. Sharma, Yogendra K., *op. cit*, p. 88.
25. *Ibid.*, p. 85.
26. *Ibid.*, pp. 89, 90, 91.
27. *Ibid.* p. 93.
28. *Ibid.* p. 75.
29. *Ibid.*, p. 75.
30. *Ibid.*, p. 78.
31. *Ibid.*, p. 80.
32. *Ibid.*, p. 80.
33. *Ibid.*, p. 80.
34. *Ibid.*, p. 81.
35. Goldstein, Sidney, (1979), Migration and Rural Development: Research Directions on Interrelations, FAO Economic and Social Development, Paper 8, FAO, Rome.
36. Gulhati, Ravi, (1978), *India's Population Polity: Critical Issues for the Future*, Reprinted from Public Policy, 26, Summer, pp. 415-54.
37. Johnson, Stanley (1973), (Ed.) *The Population Problem*, Halsted Press, New York.
38. Mehta, B.C. (1979), *Regional Population Growth:- A Case Study of Rajasthan*, Research Books, Jaipur.
39. Mohapatra, P. S., Measuring the Performance of Family Planning Programmes, World Bank, Washington D.C., Working Paper No. 257, 1977.
40. Mondot, B. and M. Jacqueline. (1977), *Relationships between Fertility, Child Mortality and Nutrition in Africa: Tentative Analysis*, OECD, Paris.
41. Pethe, Y. P. (1981), *Population Policy and Compulsion in Family. Planning*, Continental Prakashan, Poona.
42. United Nations (1981), *Population of Bangladesh*, New Work.
43. United Nations Demographic Transition and Socio-Economic Development, *Population Studies*, No. 65, 1979.
44. United Nations, Population of Nepal, New York, ESCAP Country Monograph Series 61980.

45. Adepoju, A., Population Policies in Africa: Problems and Prospects, *African Affairs*, October, 1965.
46. Cigno, A., Growth with Exhaustible Resources and Endogenous Population, *Review of Economic Studies*, April 1981.
47. Crook, N. R., On Welfare and Population Control in the Second-best World, *Economic and Political Weekly*, 12: 17-20 January, 8, 1977.
48. Eberstadt, Nick, Recent Declines in Fertility in Less Developed Countries, and What Population Planning may Learn from Them, *World Development*, Vol. 8 January, 1980 p. 37-60
49. Gwatkin, D. R., Signs of Change in Developing Country Mortality Trend: The End of an Era? Development Paper No. 30, 1-40 Overseas Development Council, Washington, February 1981.
50. Visaria, Pravin, Recent Trends in Indian Population Policy, *Economic and Political Weekly*, 11: 1187-1202, August 1976.
51. Alvarez, F. C. (1976), *New Horizons for the Third Would*, Public Affairs Press, Washington.
52. Bhatt, V. V. (1980), *Development Perspectives: Problem, Strategy and Policies*, Pergamon Press, Oxford.
53. Chenery, H. and M. Syequin (1980), *Patterns of Development, 1950-1970*, Oxford University Press, Oxford.
54. May, Brian (1981), *The Third World Calamity*, Routledge & Kegan Paul, London.
55. Sachs, Ignacy (1976), *The Discovery of the Third Would*, M.I.T. Press, Massachusetts.
56. Johnson, B. L. C. (1979), *India: Resources and Development*, Heinemann Educational Books, London.
57. Boserup, Ester (1981), *Population and Technological Change: A Study of Long-term Trends*, Chicago University Press, Chicago.
58. Brown, Lester (1974), *In the Human Interest: A Strategy to Stabilize World Population*, Norton, New York.
59. Cairnrcross, J. (1980), Population and Agriculture in the Developing Countries, FAO.
60. Cassen, R. H. (1978), *India: Population, Economy, Society*, Holmes & Meier, New York.
61. Cochrane, S. H. (1979), The Population of Thailand: Its Growth and Welfare, World Bank, Washington, D.C., Working Paper No. 337.
62. Faruquee, R. R. (1979), Sources of Fertility Decline: Factor Analysis of Inter-Country Data, World Bank, Washington, D.C., Working Paper No. 318.
63. Kocher, J. E. (1973), *Rural Development, Income Distribution and Fertility Decline*, The Population Council, New York.
64. Pearson, Karl (1911), *The Grammar Science*, A and V Black, London, p. 10.

2

Population Theories

Population has attracted the attention of a number of scholars. The germs of certain ideas, which have figured prominently in recent theoretical works on population can be found in very ancient writings. The thesis that excessive growth of population may reduce output per worker, depress the level of living of the masses and engender strife is of great antiquity.[1] Since very initial stages in the development of demographic studies of the society, demographers have been drawing attention towards population theories.[2] Confucius and other Chinese thinkers, at the very initial stages of development, realised that population explosion could dislocate economic system of a nation.[3] They observed that mortality increases when food supply is insufficient; that premature marriage leads to high infant mortality rates; that war checks population growth; and that costly marriage ceremonies reduce the marriage rate. They did not attempt to show how the variations of mortality, fertility and nuptiality as well as migration might affect the balance between population and sources.[4]

Ancient and Medieval Views on Population

Both Plato and Aristotle considered the question of optimum size of population in discussions of the ideal conditions of a City-State in which man's potentialities could be fully developed and his "highest good" realised. Their treatment of this question was by no means limited to its economic aspects. The "good life" could be attained, they believed, only if the population was large enough to be economically self-sufficient and capable of defending itself, but not too large for constitutional Government. Self-sufficiency required the possession of enough territory to cater to the need of the people and make possible a moderate level of living.[5] However, neither Plato nor Aristotle inquired explicitly into the relation between the size of the population density and per capita output or the connection between the size of the population and the opportunities for division of labour. Plato specified 5,0470 as the number of citizens "most likely, to be useful to all cities", because it has fifty-nine division "and" will burnish numbers for war and peace, and for all contracts and dealings, including taxes and division of the land.[6]

Aristotle was less specific with regard to the optimum number, but he held that unless the size of land and property could not be increased as rapidly as population would grow; civil discord would ensure, and it would be impossible for the Government to function effectively.[7]

The views of Plato and Aristotle regarding the means of controlling the size of population are noteworthy.[8] Plato proposed to restrict births, if necessary, by restraining the reproduction of those "in whom generation is affluent"; if a higher birth rate were required, he would achieve it by means of rewards, stigma, advice and rebuke to the young men from their elders. If the population grows too large in spite of these precautions, it could be reduced by colonisation and immigration, which could be used, if absolutely necessary, to replenish a population greatly diminished by wars or epidemics. Aristotle mentioned child-exposure and abortion as suitable means of preventing an excessive number of children and, in this connection, paid some attention to eugenics.[9] Both Plato and Aristotle believed that there was direct relationship between population and poverty.[10] Plato also believed that population equilibriums were necessary for maintaining social equilibrium. Herodotus, Thucydides and Xenophon, the other Greek thinkers also discussed the problems of population.

The views of the Roman thinker were different from the Greek thinker on the population. They were less conscious than the Greeks of possible limits to population growth and more alert to its advantages for military and related purposes. Perhaps partly because of this difference in outlook, Roman thinkers paid less attention than the Greeks to population theory, but were much concerned with the practical problem of stimulating population increase. Their attitude was indicated by their disapproval of celibacy, their writings in defence of marriage and procreation and by their legislation aimed at raising the marriage and birth rates.

Cicero, touching upon this subject, rejected Plato's communism in wives and children and held that the State's population must be kept up by monogamous marriage.[11] Cicero listed various checks to population growth—floods, epidemics, famines, wild animals, war, revolution, but he did not attempt to state a general theory of the determinants of population increase or decrease.

Christian writers considered the questions of population almost entirely from a moral and ethical standpoint. Since they were concerned more with the next world than with the present, they did not stress material values. Their doctrines were mainly populationist, but they placed less emphasis than earlier Hebrew and other religious writers on maxims adjuring men to multiply and people the earth.[12] On the one hand; they condemned abortion, infanticide, child-exposure, divorce, and polygamy; on the other hand, they glorified virginity and continence, considered celibacy superior to marriage though suited only to certain persons, and frowned on second marriage.

Unlike the Greeks and Romans, early medieval authors did not attach great importance to population growth as a source of strength for the State, but in time, with the reappearance of Aristotle's influence, this point was again emphasised.[13] Some medieval defenders of ecclesiastical celibacy restored to economic arguments of a vaguely proto-Malthusian character, nothing the extent to which the population of the world had grown, attributing observed poverty and want to this cause, and citing pestilence, famine, war, etc., as nature's means of pruning excess population.

The prevailing tendency, however, was to favour population increase, as it had been in earlier times. The high rates of mortality, which were found throughout the world, and the constant threat of sudden depopulation through famines, epidemics and wars predisposed ancient and medieval writers alike to favour maintenance of a high birth rate.[14]

The economic interpretation of the population size started only in the fourteenth century when the Arab scholar, Ibn Khaldun, who expounded in detail a theory of cyclical variation of population and their relation to economic, political and socio-psychological conditions. He stressed the importance of a high per capita income. According to Ibn Khaldun, a densely settled population was conducive to a better standard of living because it promoted a greater division of labour and utilisation of resources, and also ensured political stability.[15] He was of the opinion that favourable economic conditions and political stability contributed to population growth. On the other hand, economic progress encouraging luxurious living led to higher taxation and political instability, which, in turn, led to economic depression and depopulation.

Botero, an Italian of the sixteenth century, who put forth ably some of the argument later developed by Malthus.[16] Botero held that man's generative powers operate with undiminished vigor irrespective of his numbers, whereas man's capacity to produce subsistence is subject to limits. The limitation of subsistence limits population through war, strife and various secondary checks to which the struggle for a limited subsistence gives rise. Presumably, Botero believed that the limits of subsistence had been reached, and that a further increase in population could not in general augment the flow of the means of support, since he declared that the population and the supply of food had remained constant for three thousand years or longer.[17]

The mercantilist school of political economy, which flourished in Europe during much of the seventeenth and eighteenth centuries, emphasised the economic, political and military advantages of a large and growing population and favoured various measures to stimulate population growth. These measures included the imposition of disabilities on celibates; the employment of penalties, favours and monetary rewards to encourage marriage and production of large families; the removal of disabilities on illegitimate children; checks to emigration and stimuli to immigration and improvements in medicine and public health. The mercantilists paid special attention to the relation between population and foreign trade.

R. Cantillon suggested that, if the agriculture of a country could not be expanded in proportion to the population, or if such an expansion would involve diminishing returns, additional agricultural products could be obtained from abroad in exchange for manufactured good.[18] According to J. Steuart, "work" should be exported and "matter" imported so long as satisfactory terms of trade could be obtained; otherwise, population would have to be contained within the limits of home-produced subsistence.[19] Few mercantilist or cameralist writers attempted a systematic explanation of population changes, but they did discuss a variety of checks to population growth; plagues, wars accidents, uncongenial climate, infecundity due to urbanisation and other causes, vice, abortion, deferment of marriage, celibacy, monopoly, luxurious living, emigration, etc.

In England, before the mid-seventeenth century, emigration to colonies was approved on the ground that it relived population pressure at home; during the century that followed, it was sometimes condemned on the ground that it reduced the size of the domestic population. This latter view was usually rejected, however, on the ground that colonies were complementary to the mother country and that emigrants to colonies brought into being supplies and markets, which operated in time to increase the population capacity of the mother country.[20] Franklin held that the America was complementary to the British, and hence its expansion would augment the population of Britain.

The period in which mercantilism flourished saw the beginning of scientific analysis and measurement of population trends. J. Graunt observed that "the numerical deaths and births, of the ratios of the sexes at death and birth and of the proportions of deaths from certain causes to all deaths in successive years and in different areas; in general terms, the uniformity and predictability of many important biological phenomena in the mass.[21] Petty gave more stress on the advantages of the large population on fiscal, administrative and economic growth. Sussmilch, author of the first complete treatise on population, was influenced by the work of both Graunt and Petty. Sussmilch thought that population normally tended to double every century, but that the period required for doubling would lengthen as population grew. According to him, population growth could be restrained by celibacy and differed marriage and, above all, by pestilence, war, earthquakes, floods and starvation. Since he expected only advantages from population growth, therefore, he set no store by a rising standard of living and favored measures, which would accelerate growth.

The physiocratic school evolved in France when there was acute agricultural distress and misery among the people. This followed from the dominance of the mercantile policy, which led to the growth of industry at the cost of agriculture. Therefore, towards the middle of the eighteenth century, prominent thinkers, such as Quesnay and Mirabeau established a new idea that land was the source of all wealth and, thus, it was necessary that proper importance be assigned to agriculture.[22]

According to the physiocratic school, a growing and large population was good as long as agriculture could be expanded to support it. As the population was directly dependent on agriculture for food supply, any effort to suppress agriculture could, therefore, adversely affect it. The physiocratic school sees the relationship between population and the means of subsistence, which, in turn, led to the idea that agriculture should be encouraged.

Biologists, Sociologists, Economists and other thinkers have given their own views about population growth and problem of population. In our modern times, biological theories make us believe that human beings live and die in the same manner as animals and plants. Some important biological theories are as follows:

1. Michael Thomas Sadler's Destiny and Fecundity Principle
2. Diet Theory of Thomas Doubleday
3. Raymond Pearl and Lowell J. Reed's Logistic Curve Theory
4. Corridor Gini's Theory of Biological Stages
5. Herbert Spencer's Analysis of Fertility Function
6. Jouse d Castro's Theory of Protein Consumption

There are also some social and economic theories of population. Sociologist and Economist have tried to attribute growth and explosion of population to social and economic causes. According to them, population of a country is much dependent on economic and political conditions of that country on one hand and social on the other, and the both cannot be separated from each other. Some of the important theories are as following:

1. Malthusian Theory
2. Neo-Malthusian Theory
3. Surplus Population Theory of Karl Marx
4. Surplus Population and Social Mal-adjustment Theory of Henry George
5. Voluntarism by Fetter
6. Brento's Theory of Increasing Prosperity
7. Ungern Stberg's Theory of Rationalism
8. Principle of Individuality by Nitti
9. Optimum Theory
10. Theory of Demographic Transition
11. Eisenstein's Theory of Population and Economic Growth

There are biological, social and economic theories regarding population. Here, it is not possible to explain all these theories. Some theories are very important regarding population study. Therefore, those important theories are discussed in this thesis.

Malthusian Theory

One of the earliest attempts to explore the demographic-economic relationship in an explicit manner was Malthus. Malthusian theory has influenced the conceptualisation of the population problem in the developing countries as well as their initial demographic policy making.[23] Thomas Robert Malthus (1766-1834) wrote his 'Essay on Principle of Population' in 1798, when he was working as a priest. His views came to be widely known to the society in "Essay on the Principle of Population—As it affects the Future Improvement of Society, with Remarks on the Speculations of Mr. Godwin." He expressed his ideas as reactions to the views of Ricardo and Smith.

Thomas Robert Malthus modified some of his conclusions in the next famous essay in 1803, which was entitled, "An Essay on the Principle of Population or A View of Past and Present Effects on Human Happiness." His thought has become a landmark in the history of demography. He shared neither the mercantilists' craze for the big populations or the Utopians' faith in changing human nature. It was a time when it was believed that the pressure of population on earth was increasing. The Society was sharply divided between the rich and the poor. The poor were being ruthlessly exploited by the rich.

In Europe, both wars and diseases had created many horrors. Though the population was increasing, there was no increase in production. It was also a time when the Industrial Revolution took place and with that many new problems confronted the society.[24] Malthus saw with his own eyes that Industrial Revolution was making the rich richer, but the poor were becoming poorer.

The rapidly increasing population in England, encouraged by a misguided poor law, distressed Malthus very deeply. He feared that England was heading for a disaster, and he considered it his solemn duty to warn his countrymen.[25] He deplored "the strange contrast between over-care in breeding animals and carelessness in breeding men."

Malthus's argument rested upon the supposition that man's capacity to increase his means of subsistence was much less than his capacity to multiply; he asserted that man could increase his subsistence only in arithmetical progression, whereas his numbers tended to increase in geometrical progression. The history of mankind demonstrated, he said, that population always tended towards the limit set by subsistence and was contained within that limit by war, famine, pestilence, premature mortality, which were all resolvable into terms of "misery and vice", he declared, though he did describe as a check "deferment of marriage" from a foresight of the difficulties attending a following. It followed, he believed, that existing institutional and psychological barriers to marriage and population growth should not be relaxed since such relaxation would make matters even worse, but it did not follow the salutary population pressure should be eliminated were that possible.[26]

In the second and later editions of his essay, Malthus examined at greater length what he regarded as the principal cause of mass poverty, namely population pressure. The diversion of too large an amount of population is necessarily limited by the means of subsistence. Population invariably increases where the means of subsistence increase, unless prevented by some very powerful and obvious checks. He introduced a new check, "moral restraint" or the deferment of marriage by prospective spouses until they were in a position to support a family.[27] Malthus based his reasoning on the biological fact that every living organism tends to multiply to unimaginable extent. A Single pair of thrushes would multiply into 19,500,000 within the life of the first pair and 20 years later to 1,200,000,000,000,000,000,000 and if they stood shoulder to shoulder, about one in every 1,50,000 would be able to fine perching space on the whole surface of the globe.[28] According to Huxley's estimate, the descendants of a single greenfly, if all survived and multiplied, would at the end of one summer weigh down the population of China. Human beings are supposed to double every 25 year and a couple can increase to the size of the present population in 1,750 year.

According to K.K. Dewett, such is the prolific nature of every specie including man. The power of procreation is inherent and insistent, and must find expression.[29] Cantillon says, "Men multiply like mice in a barn." On the basis of these two premises, Malthus concluded that population tended to outstrip the food supply. If preventive checks, like avoidance of marriage, late marriages or less children per marriage are not exercised, the positive checks like war, famine and disease will operate.

Propositions of Malthusian Theory

The theory propounded by Thomas Robert Malthus can be reduced to the following four propositions.[30]

1. Food is necessary to the life of man and, therefore, exercises a strong check on population. In other words, population is necessarily limited by the means of subsistence, i.e., food.
2. Human population increases faster than food production. Whereas population increases in geometric progression, the food production increases in arithmetic progression.
3. Population always increases when the means of subsistence increase unless prevented by some powerful and obvious checks.
4. There are two types of checks, which can keep population on a level with the means of subsistence. They are the preventive and positive checks.

The first proposition is that the population of a country is limited by the means of subsistence. In other words, the size of population is determined by the availability of food. The greater the food production, the greater the size of production, which can be sustained. The check of deaths caused by want of food and poverty would limit the maximum possible population.

The second proposition states that the growth of population will outrun the increase in food production. Malthus thought that man's sexual urge to bear offspring knows no bounds. He seemed to think that there is no limit to the fertility of man. Man multiplies at an enormous rate. But the power of land to produce food is limited. Malthus thought that the law of diminishing returns operated in the field of agriculture and that the operation of this law put a limit on increase in the supply of food.

Malthus asserted that the population of a country tends to double every twenty-five year (as it was actually happening in the American colonies and the U.K. at that time), but the food supply could be increased much less rapidly. In fact, Malthus observed that the population tended to increase at a geometric rate—2, 4, 8, 16, 32, 64, etc., but the food supply tended to increase at an arithmetic rate—2, 4, 6, 8, 10, 12. Thus at the end of two hundred years, "The ratio of population to the means of subsistence would be 259 to 9; in three centuries, it would be 4,096 to 13; and in two thousand years, the difference would be incalculable." Therefore, Malthus asserted that the population would ultimately outstrip the food supply. For this reason, Malthus said that people were doomed forever to live at a bare subsistence level. When food supply runs short, people must starve and be plunged into misery.

The third proposition is that as the food supply in a country increases, the people will produce more children and would have larger families. This would increase the demand for food and the availability of food per person will again diminish. Therefore, according to Malthus, the standard of living of the people cannot rise permanently, unless they exercised restraints and limited the size of family.

In the fourth proposition, the control of population. Malthus suggested to check population growth through preventive checks and positive checks.

Checks on Population

According to Malthus, there were two possible checks, which controlled the growth of population. These checks are as following.[31]

1. Preventive Checks: Preventive checks exercise their influence on the growth of population by bringing down the birth rate. They are applied by man himself. They arise from man's wisdom and foresight. He sees the distress, which frequently visits those who have large families. He may think that with a large number of children, the standard of living of the family may be lowered. He may think that if he has to supply for a large family, he will have to face greater difficulties and work harder than before, otherwise, he and his family would suffer. He may not be able to give adequate education to his children if there are many of them. Further, he may expose his children to poverty or to charity by his inability to provide for them. These considerations may force man to limit his family. Late marriage and self-restraint during married life are the examples of preventive checks applied by man to limit the size of his family.

2. Positive Checks: Positive checks exercise their influence on the growth of population by increasing the death rate. They are applied by nature as distinguished from preventive checks, which are exercised by man. The positive checks to population are many and include every cause, whether arising from vice or misery, which in any degree contributes to shorten the natural duration of human life. Unhealthy occupations, hard labour, exposure to the inclemencies of weather, extreme poverty, bad nursing of children, epidemics, wars and famines are some of the examples of positive checks. They all shorten human life and increase the death rate.

Malthus recommended the use of preventive checks if mankind was to escape from the impending misery. If preventive checks were not effectively used, positive checks like diseases, wars and famines would come into operation. As a result, the population would be reduced to the level, which can be sustained by the available quantity of food supply.

Malthus laid a great stress on the role of positive checks in keeping the population under control. The following remarks made by him in the first edition of his book show the way in which his mind was working,[32] "Famine seems to be the last resort, the most dreadful resource of nature. The power of population is so superior to the power of earth to provide subsistence that premature death must in some shape or the other visit the human race."

In later editions of his book,[33] Malthus softened the harshness of his theory and gave preventive checks a little more importance. Thus, he held out some hope for the human race through the operation of preventive checks in reducing the birth rate. But, he still remained firm in his pessimistic view. He put little faith in self- restraint and late marriages, since he was of the opinion that sex urge among people was very strong. Moreover, in these later editions, Malthus also maintained that increase in population would exceed the growth in food supply and if un-checked by the use of preventive checks, excessive population would lead to the operation of positive checks to take away the surplus population.

Malthus has given his ideas about some other aspects of population as well. According to him, migration of population was likely to solve, at least temporarily, food problem of a country. Emigration of population is to the advantage of poor nations on food front. He also believed that specialisation in agriculture and production of finished goods can be useful for a nation, but at the same time, it need not be forgotten that those nations, which are industrially and commercially advanced, can purchase food from agriculturally advanced nations to the extent they need.

Criticism of Malthus's Theory

Malthus's theory has been criticised on various accounts. In fact, his theory raised a big controversy not during his own times, but still remains open to criticism. Prof Marshal, Trussing, Coosa, Ely Patten and Carver were the prominent supporters of his theory, whereas his theory was criticised by Oppenheim, Graham and others. Prof Gray is of the view that his theory raised such a big controversy that almost every important thinker paid attention to what he said. It was, however, unfortunate that he was too much vilified. In his own words, "It is to say that no respectable citizen has ever been so vilified and abused as Malthus, no writer of the first magnitude has been so often refuted." The following are some of the important grounds on which he has been criticised:

1. It is pointed out that Malthus's pessimistic conclusions have not been borne out by the history of Western European Countries. The gloomy forecast made by Malthus about the miserable conditions of future generations of mankind has not proved true in the Western World. Whereas population has failed to grow as rapidly as predicted by Malthus, production has increased tremendously because of the rapid advances in technology. As a result, living standards of the people have risen instead of falling as was predicted by Malthus.
2. The Malthusian theory is based on the law of diminishing returns as applied to agriculture. It is on the basis of this law that Malthus asserted that food production could not keep pace with population growth. By making rapid advances in technology and larger application of capital, advanced countries have been able to postpone the stage of diminishing returns. By making use of fertilizers, better seeds, tractors and other agricultural machinery, they have been able to increase their production greatly. In fact, in most of the advanced countries, the rate of increase of food production has been much greater than the rate of population growth. Thus, inventions and improvements in the methods of production have failed the gloomy forecast of Malthus by holding the law of diminishing returns in check almost indefinitely.

3. Malthus considered food production alone and not the production of wealth in its forms. He compared the population growth with the increase in food production alone. Malthus held that since land was limited in quantity, food production could not increase faster than population. But, he should have taken into account all types of production in considering the question of the optimum size of the population. England did feel the shortage of land and food. If England had been forced to support its population entirely from her own soil, there can be little doubt that England would have experienced series of famines by which its growth of population would have been checked.

   But England did not experience any such disaster. It is because England industrialised itself by developing its natural resources other than land like coal and iron, and by accumulating man-made capital equipments, like factories, tools, machines, mines, ships and railways. This enabled it to produce plenty of industrial and manufactured goods, which it then exported in exchange for food-stuffs from foreign countries. There is, thus, no food problem in England. Thus, Malthus made a mistake in taking agricultural land and food production alone into account while discussing the population question. He should have considered all types of production instead.

4. Malthus held that the increase in the means of subsistence or food supplies will cause population to grow so fast that ultimately means of subsistence or food supply will be in level with population and everyone would get only bare minimum subsistence. In other words, according to Malthus, living standards of the people cannot rise in the long run above the level of minimum subsistence. But as already pointed out, living standards of the people in the Western world have risen greatly and stand much above the minimum subsistence level. There is no evidence of birth-rate rising with the increase in the standard of living. Instead, there is ample evidence that birth rates fall as prosperity grows.

   In the Western countries, the attitude towards children changed as they prospered. Previously, much attention was not paid to children. But now parents feel a duty to do as much as they can for each child and, therefore, they decide not to have more children than they can attend to. People now care more for higher standard of living than rearing more children. The extensive use of contraceptives and change in the attitude towards children in the Western World has brought down the birth rate in that region. This change in the attitude towards children and the wider use of contraceptives in the Western World have falsified Malthusian doctrine.

5. Malthus gave no proof of his assertion that population increased exactly in an arithmetic progression. It has been rightly pointed out that population and food supply do not change in accordance with these mathematical series. The growth of population and food supply cannot be expected to show the precision or accuracy of such series. However, Malthus, in later editions of his book, did not insist on these mathematical terms and only held that there was an inherent tendency in population to outrun the means of subsistence. It has been observed that even this is far from true.
6. Malthus has tried to establish that increasing population among the poor and downtrodden of the society is responsible for the poverty of society. It is, therefore, most desirable that the poor should not marry so that population growth is checked. There is considerable element of truth in the saying that it cannot be denied that growth of population among the poor is not under the control of the State, resulting in the concentration of economic power in the hands of a few only. It shows that Malthus has not gone too deep into the causes of poverty and has superficially analysed the whole problem.
7. Prof. Gide has criticised Malthus in his way. According to him, Malthus has not been proved very correct in his prophecy. In his own words that history certainly has not confirmed his fears. No single country has shown that it is sufferings from over-population. In some cases, that of France for example, population has increased only very slightly.
8. While expounding his theory, Malthus has taken it for granted that the whole world is vegetarian and requires food of that kind. He has forgotten that a large part of the world is purely non-vegetarian and does not need vegetarian food, but eats fish, meat, etc. This population does not affect food

production. There are some parts of the world where people do not at all depend on staple food.

9. Prof. Haney is of the view that Malthus was simply influenced by his surroundings and under their influence, he only expounded his theory. In his own words, "He knew what happened, he saw what was happening, but influenced by his surroundings, his vision as to what was to happen, was unduly obscured."
10. Karl Marx has rather very harshly criticised Malthus for expounding his theory. According to him, "Malthus was altogether a plagiarist by profession. He borrowed nonsense from earlier writers, like Rev. Townsend. His geometric and arithmetical progressions were purely chimerical hypotheses. He copied and paraphrased Rev. Townsend like a slavish plagiarist."
11. Malthus has been criticised both by Winston Churchill and Henry Villard. Both of them are of the view that a stage is bound to come when growth of population rate will automatically be checked and not go on the basis of geometrical progression.

Importance of Malthus's Theory

Though Malthus has been much criticised for his theory, yet it is wrong to think that he was without any basis. In fact, there are many elements of truth in his theory. The very fact that his theory has been so seriously studied all over the world and drew the attention of almost every important thinker of his time proves that the theory was of great significance and importance. In the words of Prof. Walker, "Malthusianism has stood unsheltered importance amid all the controversy that has raged around it. Then it has been pointed out that the critics have tried to discuss the theory keeping in view conditions of only one country at a time. It cannot be denied that if production of all the countries of the world on the one hand and that of the food supplies on the other is taken, then it will have to be accepted that for unlimited population, there is always limited food-supply.[34] Then, another importance of the theory is that whatsoever Malthus has said during his own times holds good even today in so far as developing and underdeveloped nations are concerned. In these countries, the rate of population growth is definitely much faster than that of food production Russell said, "Malthus statement of population has been true enough up to the time when he wrote. It is still true of the barbarous and semi-civilised races and of the most elements among the civilised nations."

Then, it has been pointed out that even today the fundamentals of Malthus theory remain unchanged and these have not been refuted in any manner. As Prof. Walker has pointed out that the fact remains that in every society every person is trying to increase his requirements of life, which put additional burden on available food resources. Moreover, there are only very few people, who can check their family size according to their food resources. Normally, family grows in the hope that efforts will be made to procure food once the child has been born. Once family size begins to increase, then there is no end to it. Thus, it cannot be belied that Malthus has given a theory, which is basically sound and that the rate of population growth is much faster than that of the food production.

The Malthusian theory fully applies to countries like India. India is at present in that unenviable position, which Malthus feared. We have the highest birth-rate and the highest death-rate in the world. Grinding poverty, ever-recurring epidemics, famine, communal quarrels are the order of day. We are deficient in food supply. Our standard of living is incredibly low. Who can say that Malthus was not a true prophet; if not for his country, at any rate, his theory was true for countries like India and China.[35]

The Population division of United Nations has mentioned the Malthus contribution in its article.[36] According to this article, Malthus contribution to the development of population theory was far greater than his writings reveal. His essay aroused a storm of controversies, which outlived Malthus himself and which made both his followers and his opponents conscious of the need for adequate information about population trends and for painstaking investigation of their relations with social and economic conditions. Thus, Malthus was indirectly responsible for a large measure of the progress, which has been made since his time in development population Censuses and a vital statistics, improving the techniques of demographic analysis and formulation of better grounded population theories.

Though Malthusian theory has been criticised, yet his basic principle that population growth should be checked is today very much championed by the propagators of family planning programmes. Today, no nation in the world can say that it wants to have unlimited population because each nation has limited economic and other sources.

Neo-Malthusian Theory

Recently, Neo-Malthusian theory has come to the front. These thinkers have faith that whatsoever Malthus said about population growth was absolutely correct. Neo-Malthusians believed that without any effect on the sexual pleasure of the couple, the growth of population should be checked. This should be done with the help of recent devices and methods.[37] Neo-Malthusian found its origin as early as in 1884 when Dr. Drysdale brought out his famous book entitled, 'Elements of Social Science.' In Neo-Malthusianism, doctors, social scientists, political and economists all showed keen interest. All of them distinguished between desire for sex and that of producing children. In 1887, some of them founded the Malthusian league. They propagated that use of contraceptives was very useful for checking population growth and that there was no harm in that.

Neo-Malthusians make a distinction between desire for sex and also the desire for having children. According to them, sex desire is something natural, whereas desire to produce children is based on religious, social and cultural considerations. In the words of Prof. Gide, "The first is more animal instinct, which arouses more impetuous of passions and is common to all men. The second is frequently social and religious in origin assuming different forms according to exigencies of time and place."

The Hindus, as we know, want to have children on religious ground because according to them, a childless couple is likely to go to hell. The Muslims want to increase their tribe whereas the poor want children in the hope that they might get more earning hands, etc.[38] Neo- Malthusians point out that in our modern society, the number of such persons, who want to enjoy sexual life, but do not wish to have any children is very considerably increasing. In fact, these days, due to materialism, sex desire is far more than what it was in the past. The people do not want children because responsibilities towards them are very rapidly increasing, and there is also the desire to save themselves from deterioration of health, which is bound to be true due to pangs of delivery and so on.

Neo-Malthusians believe that no one should suppress sex urge because that is natural. In case any attempt is made to suppress such an urge that is bound to create mental agony in the minds of the people. There is, then, every possibility that the people may like to follow evil practices. As we know that in every society those who do not find natural methods of satisfying sex desire, follow unholy and unnatural methods, thereby creating many social and law and order problems.

Neo-Malthusians believe that there is no harm in using contraceptives because with their use, human beings can satisfy their sexual urge without producing children. They also believe that birth control is the most essential for all the sections of society. They also believe that with the help of modern scientific means and methods, it is possible to check population growth and increase food production in proportion to population growth.

Neo-Malthusians have been criticised on many accounts as well. It is said that if the use of contraceptives or similar other methods for checking of population are followed, then women-folk will miserably suffer mentally, morally and physically. Their health as well as physique and mental outlook will receive a serious setback. The use of these things can result in many diseases among the women. In case these are extensively used, then there is a danger that even a race might be wiped out all together. Bertrand Resell, while discussing the whole issue has said that, "What is regrettable at present is not the decline of the birth rate in itself, but the fact that decline is the greatest in the best elements of the population.

Theory of Optimum Population

Modern economists have rejected the Malthusian theory of maximum population, which if exceeded, will spell misery in the country. Instead of the maximum population, the modern economists have substituted the idea of optimum population.[39] The theory of optimum population is comparatively a new theory in so for as theories are concerned.

Sir Edwin Cannon, however, used the term optimum and presented his idea about population in his Optimum Theory of Population. He also gave its scientific explanation at some length. In our modern times, Prof. Dalton and Prof. Robbins have discussed this theory at some length. It is today everywhere accepted that every country must conceive an optimum population and should not allow their population to go beyond that.[40]

Optimum population means the ideal number of the population that a country should have, considering its resources. It means the best and the most desirable size of a country's population. It is the right number. When a country's population is neither too big nor too small, but just that much, which the country ought to have, it is called the optimum population. Given a certain amount of resources, state of technical knowledge and a certain stock of goods and services, the per capita income will be the highest. This is the optimum size. The optimum number can, therefore, be defined as the one at which per capita income is the highest.

Following are the important definitions of optimum[41] population.[42]

1. *Prof. Alexander Carr Saunders*: "The optimum population is that population, which produces maximum economic welfare. Maximum economic welfare is not necessarily the same as maximum real income per head, but for practical purposes, they may be taken as equivalent."
2. *K.E. Boulding*: "The population at which the standard of life is at maximum is called the optimum population."
3. *Dr. Dalton*: "Optimum population is that which gives the minimum income per head."
4. *Prof. Robbins*: "The population which just makes the maximum return possible is the optimum or the best possible population."
5. *Prof Cannon*: At any given time (in a country) there is what may be called a point of maximum return, when the amount of labour is such that both an increase and decrease in it would diminish proportionate returns. If population is not large enough to bring all industry up to this point, returns will be less than they might be and remedy is increase of population; if on the other hand, population is so great that point has been passed, returns are again less than they might be and the remedy is decrease in population."

Though different scholars have tried to define optimum production in their own way, yet all of them agree that optimum population of a country is that which helps in maximum production with the help of other natural resources of the country. In other words, it is a point at which per capita income is the maximum and the production is the maximum.

While understanding the concept of optimum population, it is necessary to know the concepts of under-population and over-population.

Under-population

If the population of a country is below the optimum, i.e., below what it ought to be, then the country is said to be under-populated. The number of people is insufficient to take the fullest possible advantage of the natural and capital resources of the country. This is what happens in a new country. The resources are vast. Much can be produced, but there are not enough people to carry on the work of production efficiently.[43]

Apart from the insufficiency of working force, the disadvantages arise from the difficulty of specialisation owing to less numbers. By specialisation, workers acquire job dexterity and increased efficiency in the use of specialised equipments. The community will not be able to reap the benefits of large scale production. Thus, production would suffer.[44]

Under such conditions, an increase in population will be followed by an increase in the per capita income. But this increase cannot go on indefinitely When the shortage of man-power has been made up, the per capita income will reach the maximum, and we shall say that optimum has been reached.

Over-population

If however, the population still goes on increasing and the optimum is exceeded, then we shall have a state of over–population; there will be too many people in the country. The country's resources will not be sufficient to provide gainful employment to all. Because of this, the per capita income will diminish; standard of living will fall, famine and disease will be constant companions of such a people. These are the symptoms of over-population.[45] Capital formation will be hampered and economic development will be slowed down. The dangers of over-population, however, can be avoided by increasing the supply of capital. There is a race between productivity and population. If productivity wins the race, the danger is averted.

To the Optimum

Suppose that natural resources, stock of capital equipment and state of technology remain fixed in a country. Now assume that the population, which was initially very small relative to these other resources, begins to increase. With the increase in population, labour force of the country will also increase. As more and more labour is combined with fixed amounts of these other resources, output per capita or real income per head will rise,[46] because the increase in the equality of labour will make possible greater degree of specialisation and more efficient use of natural and capital resources of the country. With a very small population or labour force, there would be limited scope for specialisation, for each worker would be required to do all sorts of jobs.

But as population and, therefore, the quantity of labour increases, specialisation becomes possible. Each man then need not do all the jobs or make all parts of a good. Everybody can concentrate on the job for which he is best suited. Division of labour among different workers, which is made possible by the increase in population, would greatly increase the efficiency and productivity of labour.

An increase in population will also permit a fuller utilisation of natural resources and capital equipment.[47] If the quantity of labour is small relative to the natural resources, then even the actually available resources remain under utilised. Many actually available resources, which can be utilised for producing goods, would not be utilised for lack of labour. Moreover, even the capital equipment will not be fully and effectively utilised if there is a shortage of labour. Technology requires that capital equipment be of a certain minimum size whether output is relatively small or large. Capital equipment would not be fully utilised if only a small number of workers are available to work with it. In other words, production will be relatively inefficient if the capital equipment is grossly undermanned. If the population increases and more laborers become available to be combined with the given stock of the natural resources and capital equipment, the output per capita will rise.

Thus, both under-population and over-population have disadvantages. It is the optimum population with the highest per capita output, which is the best for a country to aim it.

Size of Population: Optimum, Over and Under Population

Criteria of Over-Population

There are several criteria of over-population. According to Malthus, the operation of positive checks likes war, famine and disease is a sure index of a country being over-populated. Besides this, economists generally suggest several other tests of over-population, i.e. persistently unfavourable balance of trade, unemployment, falling living standards and average income, and high birth and death rates.[48] But a little reflection will show that these phenomena may not always be caused by overflowing numbers, but by other factors—economic and political.

This cannot offer any infallible guide to the state of over-population. All the same, a continued state of under-employment, ill-health and poverty are fairly correct indications of the fact that ever growing numbers are over-straining the country's slender resources.

In India, we find ourselves at present in this unenviable position of over-population. How can we now get back to the optimum? We must attack the problem by accelerating the pace of our economic development.[49] Our is country of unutilised or underutilised resources. The execution of multi-purpose projects, and the development of agriculture, industry, insurance and banking and of the means of transport, etc., steps in this direction. When we try to keep down our numbers and maximise our productive capacity, we shall be on the road to the optimum.

Criticism of the Optimum Theory

Though the theory of optimum population is definitely an improvement on the theory expounded by Malthus, yet the critics have pointed out certain important defects in the theory. This has considerably lowered practical utility and value of the theory. Some of the main points of criticism are following.[50]

1. Optimum theory of population can help in finding out what was the population of a country at a given point of time or that when a population is optimum, below or above that. But the theory does not tell us as to why and how the population of the country increased or decreased. Every

important theory of population must deal with this aspect of the problem.

2. In this theory, maximum stress has been laid on population, but the theory has almost ignored distribution, which is equally important. Who does not know that for collective welfare of society, distribution, no less important than production, is bound to result in the concentration of wealth in the hands of a few persons. Then, it is possible that per capita income might show an increase, but the people still might be miserable.
3. The theory of optimum population proceeds on the presumption that whereas population grows slowly and steadily, there is very little change in the habits of the people, tastes and technical know-how, but it is not true. We know that economic position and situation continues to change and is never stable. Technical know–how, etc. continuously change with the result that people of different skills and caliber become in acute need at different time. It is not in fact sound to call any population as optimum or ideal.
4. Another defect is that this theory has adopted a very materialistic outlook. In this, capital or wealth has been given a place and position. It is believed in this theory that per capita income should remain the highest and that maximum income is the only indication of progress of society. But again, this theory has faltered. We know that all do want not maximum wealth, but certainly happiness. Wealth is not an end in itself, but only means to an end; wealth is needed for happiness and not for sorrows and miseries.
5. It is also criticised that this theory has not touched social and political aspects of life in a society and the role, which they play in the national life. These are situations, which economically might appear favourable, but politically, these might not be accepted or vice-versa. During war, maximum manpower is needed and political bosses will certainly cherish regular supply of manpower to win the war, no matter whether living standard of the people goes up or not.
6. The critics point out that it is a pity that optimum theory of population has not touched such important aspects of population as nature and role of sole distributors, pertinent to the determination of population size. It also does not deal

with fields of action that can conceivably pertain to the process of demographic and economic change. The theory has failed to discuss the role of values in the determination of population size on the one hand and behaviour equations that lead to different population sizes. In fact, the theory has been badly criticised by some leading social scientists. Hauser and Duncan are of the view that this theory is static and volatile. Hicks is of the opinion that it is a nation of extremely little practical use. Brimley Thomas is of the view that the whole concept is shadowy and elusive.

Theory of Demographic Transition

The process of economic development, which has transformed agrarian economics into urban, industrialised and market-oriented economics, has led to the emergence of a new theory, the theory of demographic transition.[51] The course of population growth since Malthus has been different from what he predicted. This course is more correctly described by this new theory. The theory of demographic transition brings out the relation between population growth and economic development.

Before economic development, an economy is characterised, among other things, by predominance of agriculture, small-scale industries using inefficient and old techniques of production, lack of mobility and division of labour, lack of adequate means of transport and communication, low levels of output and average income, a high degree of rural self-sufficiency and the existence of subsistence economy. But the outstanding feature, from the population point of view, is the prevalence of high birth rates, which are stable at a high level, and high mortality rates.[52] The birth rates are high owing to universal and early marriage, the influence of social beliefs and customs, religious attitudes and, above all, from economic necessity. This is so because children start working early and thus supplement the family income and because they are regarded as a sort of insurance against old age. The birth rates are also high because the death rates are high, a family must have more children to fill up the gaps caused by high death rates.

The death rates are high owing to poor diet, bad sanitary conditions, and absence of preventive and curative medical practices. High birth rates and high death rates prevalent in an under-development economy are well in sync with the Malthusian Theory of population. In fact, high death rate is essential to prevent a population explosion, which may be caused by high birth rates. The result is that population growth is not rapid, but this is achieved through suffering, disease and death. In an agrarian economy, birth rates are stable at a high level, but death rates fluctuate from year to year, depending on availability of food and prevalence of disease.

It is necessary to see how the situation is affected by the process of development and the social and economic changes, which this development brings about. Economic development brings about an improvement in the economic condition of the people. The level of employment and productivity rises bringing about a rise in the level of living. The rural self-sufficiency is broken; the market is extended and comes to dominate production. The economy becomes industrialised and urbanised; it uses more capital and capital equipment, i.e., elaborate tools and machinery. There are rapid changes in the techniques of production. The means of transport and communication are extended and improved.

The striking trend in population in a development economy is that death rates start declining. This follows an improvement in the standard of living and the availability of medical facilities.[53] The food supply is more abundant and regular; there is greater security of life and property owing to improvement in the law and order situation. The medical innovations and the development of vaccines, antibiotics and insecticides and the improvement in sanitary conditions have eradicated many dangerous and fatal diseases. The public health measures have increasingly become more effective. The cumulative effect of all these development is to reduce substantially the incidence of disease and death. There is, thus, an increasingly pervasive pattern of rapid decline in death rates in all developing economics.

However, the birth rates prove to be more intractable. They are not so readily responsive to economic improvement. They are governed more by deeply established customs and institutions. Also, there is a general consensus in favour of reducing death and disease, but there is no such consensus supporting the desirability of small families. Thus, for a time, while the death rates have fallen, the birth rates continue to rule high, so that during the stage of incipient economic development, population growth is accelerated rather than diminished; there is rather a population explosion.[54] There is a time lag before the reduction in birth rates follows the reduction in death rates. This is what is happening in India at present.

But when a very high stage of economic development is reached as in the West, the birth rates fall too. There is deliberate limitation of the size of the family and this is facilitated by a widespread use of efficient contraceptive devices.[55] The changing structure of production involves a declining importance of the family as a production unit, where woman come to play an increasing role outside the home and where economic mobility can better be achieved with a small family. The children are considered more burden than an asset. The economic advantages of a large family disappear and the fashion of having a small family first catches the higher strata of society, but gradually infiltrates to the sections at the lower end of the economic scale and spreads eventually to the rural areas.

Thus, the birth rates decline too and establish a parallel with the decline in death rates so that the population growth slows down. Small family and low mortality become a typical pattern.

It may, however, be borne in mind that some countries like Malaysia and Sri Lanka have reduced their death rates merely through public health measures without abandoning their agrarian structure. Also, more urbanisation does not lead to reduction in fertility. In India and Egypt, for example, the differential fertility between the rural and urban sectors is practically non-existent.[56]

Thus, substantial economic improvement may be a sufficient condition for decline in mortality, but it is not today a necessary condition.[57] The relation between economic development and fertility is even less certain. Small economic changes may not reduce birth rates. In many under-developed countries, social and economic changes that are now going on are not likely to reduce fertility in the next two or three decades. The theory of demographic transition does not say what conditions are essential for fertility decline and what precisely is the period during which this decline must take place.

The theory of demographic transition has been summarised as following.[58] The agrarian low-income economy is characterised by high birth and death rates—the birth rates are relatively stable and the death rates fluctuate in response to varying fortunes. Then as the economy changes its form to a more inter-dependant and specialised market oriented economy, the average death rates decline. It continues to decline under the impact of better organisation and improving medical knowledge and care. Somewhat later, the birth rate begins to fall. The two rates follow a more or less parallel downward course with decline in birth rate lagging behind. Finally, as further reductions in the death rate become harder to attain, the birth rate again approaches equality with death rate and a more gradual growth is re-established with, however, low risks of mortality and small family as the typical pattern. Mortality rates are now relatively stable from year to year and birth rates are now responsive to voluntary decisions rather than to deeply imbedded customs, and they may fluctuate from year to year.

Thus, the Malthusian theory, Neo-Malthusian theory, Optimum Population theory and theory of Demographic Transition are discussed here. While studying these theories, it was realised that these theories are very important in the field of population.

ENDNOTES

1. Spengler, Joseph; J. and Duncan Otis Dubley (1956), (Edited) *Population Theory and Policy* (Article - History of Population Theories by the Population Division, United Nations). The Free Press, Glencoe, Illinois, USA, p. 6.
2. Raj, Hans (1993), *Population Studies*, Surjeet Publications, Delhi, p. 131.
3. *Ibid*, p. 131.
4. Huan Chang, C. (1911), *The Economic Principles of Confucius and his School*, Vol. I, pp. 180, 186.
5. Spengler, Joseph J. and Duncan Otis Dudley (1956), (Edited) Population Theory and Policy, *The Free Press*, Glencoe, Illinois, USA, p. 6.
6. *Ibid*, p. 6.
7. *Ibid*, p. 6.
8. *Ibid*, p. 6.
9. *Ibid*, p. 6, 7.
10. Raj, Hans (1993), *Population Studies*, Surjeet Publications, Delhi, p. 131.
11. Cicero (1913), *De re Publica* (Ca. 44 B.C.; 1913 edited), B.K IV, Para 5.
12. Spengler, Joseph J. and Duncan Otis Dubley (1956), (Edited) Population Theory and Policy, *The Free Press*, Glencoe, Illinois, USA, p. 7.
13. *Ibid*, p. 7.
14. *Ibid*, p. 7.
15. United Nations (1974), *The Determinants and Consequences of Population Trends*, Vol. 1, New York, p. 606.
16. United Nations, *op. cit..* p. 35.
17. United Nations, *op. cit.*, pp. 35, 36.

18. Cantillon, R. (1952), *Essai Sur la Nature du Commerce en General* (1755; 1952 edited), Chapters 15, 16.
19. Steuart, J., *An Enquiry into the Principles of Political Economy* (1767) Bk. 2, Chapters 24, 25.
20. Knorr, K. E., *British Colonial Theories*, pp. 41-48.
21. Willcox, W. F., J. (1939), Graunt's Natural and Political Observations made upon the Bill of Mortality (1662; 1939 edited) p. XII of introductory chapter.
22. Tripathy, Kamala Kanta (1993), *Population and Development*, Manak Publications Pvt. Ltd., Delhi, p. 41.
23. Tripathy, Kamala Kanta, *op. cit.* p. 42.
24. Raj, Hans, *op. cit*, p. 134.
25. Dewett, K. K. (1997), *Modern Economic Theory*, Shyamlal Charitable Trust, Delhi, p. 110.
26. Spengler, Joseph J. and Duncan Otis Dudley, *op. cit.*, p. 11, 12.
27. *Ibid*, p. 12.
28. Dewett, K. K., *op. cit.*, p. 110.
29. *Ibid*, p. 110.
30. *Ibid*, p. 110, 111.
31. *Ibid*, p. 111.
32. Malthus, Thomas Robert - An Essay on the Principle of Population; 1798 - Quoted by K. K. Dewett in his book, *Modern Economic Theory* (1997), Shyamlal Charitable Trust, Delhi.
33. Malthus, Thomas Robert, An Essay on the Principle of Population or a View of its Past and Present Effects on Human Happiness; 1803 - quoted by K. K. Dewett.
34. Raj, Hans, *op. cit.*, p. 140.
35. Dewett, K. K., op cit., pp. 112, 113.
36. History of Population Theory, Population Division, United Nations, New York, 1953.
37. Raj, Hans. *op. cit.*, p. 141.
38. *Ibid*, p. 142.
39. Dewett K. K., *op. cit.*, p. 113.
40. Raj, Hans, *op. cit.l* p. 145.
41. Dewett, K. K., *op. cit.*, p. 113.
42. Raj, Hans, *op. cit.*, p. 146.
43. Dewett, K. K., *op. cit.*, p. 113.
44. *Ibid*, p. 113.
45. *Ibid*, p. 113.
46. *Ibid*, p. 113.
47. *Ibid*, p. 113.

48. *Ibid*, p. 115.
49. *Ibid*, p. 115.
50. Raj, Hans, *op. cit.*, p. 153, 154.
51. Dewett, K. K., *op. cit.*, p. 117.
52. *Ibid*, p. 117.
53. *Ibid*, p. 117.
54. *Ibid*, p. 117.
55. *Ibid*, p. 117, 118.
56. *Ibid*, p. 118.
57. *Ibid*, p. 118.
58. Coale and Hoover (1958), *Population Growth and Economic Development in Low Income Countries*, p. 13.

3

Dr. B.R. Ambedkar's Views on Birth Control

Dr. Babasaheb Ambedkar was a man of multifaceted personality and versatile genius. There were no subjects left in the world, which Dr. Ambedkar didn't study. Agriculture and agriculturists in general, agricultural labourer's problems, industries and industrial workers, population problem and poverty were the subjects that interested him a lot. He was also very much sympathetic towards the women folk, who were subjected to manhandling and harassment. For the eradication of these problems, he was instrumental in passing the Hindu Code Bill, where he made legal provisions about the father's property, right to adopt child, etc. In this way, he has shown that the key role of women in the development of the society and a nation is very much important. Hence, later he came to be known as the emancipator of women.

Dr. Babasaheb Ambedkar was well ahead of his time and made several historical efforts to improve the living conditions of the common man and social equity. He always thought for the welfare of human being and followed the path of Lord Buddha—"Welfare of many and happiness of many."

Dr. Ambedkar was a man of action. He believed in worth and not birth. He was a man, who made tremendous efforts to change the cultural frame of India, to make suitable repercussions on cultural and demographic fronts for bringing about the much needed stimulation in economic and social development.[1]

Pressure of Population: Small Holdings and Poverty

Dr. Ambedkar was the first political leader in India, who realised the dangers of unchecked growth of population, particularly in a developing country like India. Being an eminent economist and statesman, he could understand the real crux of the problem of population economics.

Dr. Ambedkar had written an article on 'Small Holdings in India and their Remedies', which was published in the Journal of the Indian Economics Society in 1918. In this article, he mentioned how the problem of small holding is related with the population. According to him, "A large agricultural population with the lowest proportion of land in actual cultivation means that large part of the agricultural population is superfluous and idle."[2] He argued, "The grievance (of small holding) lies in the circumstances, which put a premium on these small pieces of land. The premium is no doubt to the large population depending solely on agriculture to eke out its living. Naturally, a population that has little else to prefer to agriculture will try to invoke every possible cause to get a piece of land, however small. It is not, therefore, the law of inheritance that is the evil, but it is the high pressure (of population) on land, which brings it into operation.[3]

Dr. Ambedkar pointed out the main causes of small holding. According to him, lack of alternative means of subsistence and large population are the causes, which made the existence of enlarged and consolidated holding of a particular size impossible.

Dr. Ambedkar was interviewed by leading newspaper, *The Times of India,* dated 15 August 1936, wherein he explained the aims and objectives of the Independent Labour Party. Dr. Ambedkar pointed out that the party would have its roots in the electorate and its members, who would contest the election as such, would take the pledge to the electorate to uphold a common and clearly defined programme and to be bound by the rules of discipline framed by the party.[4]

In the aims and objectives of the Independent Labour Party, Dr. Ambedkar mentioned programmes, such as economic, social reform, rural reconstruction, education and administration.

Twelve-point programme was suggested to solve the economic problems. The title of the twelve-point programme was "Pressure of Population".

Dr. Ambedkar was thinking seriously over the extreme problem of poverty prevailing in the society. In his opinion, poverty is the birth place of all ills. Therefore, he suggested several proposals to eliminate poverty. In the election manifesto of Independent Labour Party, he mentioned that the real causes of poverty among the farmers were the division of farming lands and growing population.

According to Dr. Ambedkar, the fragmentation of land holding is a severe handicap in the way of the application of capital and improved methods of cultivation to agriculture and is, therefore, a direct cause of the poverty of the agriculturists.[5] He believes that the fragmentation of land holding and the consequent poverty of the agriculturists are mainly due to the pressure of population on land and unless the pressure is relieved by draining off the excess population subsisting on land, fragmentation will continue, and the condition of the agriculturist will remain as poverty-stricken as it is today.[6]

Speaking on the budget in the Legislative Assembly on 2 March 1938, Dr. Ambedkar had rightly pointed out, "I do maintain and I state it emphatically that one of the principal duties of this Government must be to tackle the problem of poverty. The Government must see that they do adopt ways and means whereby the national income of this province rises to some substantial level, whereby the majority of the people can live in amenities, which rightly belong to all modern and civilised men. The system of social services, which has so far prevailed in European countries, whereby the Government gives what are called doles on unemployment benefit, maternity benefit and so on presupposes one thing: it presupposes that a majority of the people are above want, are above the line of poverty, and that it is only those few who, either by the vagaries of the economic system or by any misfortune befalling them, fall below the line of poverty that need assistance from the Government. It is, therefore, perfectly possible, perfectly justifiable, for European Government not to bother with the problems of general economic uplift of the people as a whole, but the problems with which we are faced in this country are of a totally different character.[7]

Dr. Ambedkar had been interested in eradicating poverty of the nation. Therefore, he suggested various measures for the eradication of poverty. While speaking on the budget, he gave stress on how to tackle the problem of poverty by the Government. Government has not taken effective measures for the eradication of poverty. Hence, in the speech on budget he said, "I have no hesitation in saying and I do not suppose there is anybody in this House who would quarrel with me if I state it, that we are all a nation of beggars and coolies. That is the description, which one can give to all this mass of people. Therefore, no Government worthy of its name can sit silent and not take account of this grave problem."[8]

Dr. Ambedkar has given the picture of poverty while discussing the issue of budget.

In recent years, eminent economist like David Maclel have emphasised on the role of basic values in promoting economic development. Eisenstein has indicated that an important suppressing factor stimulated by economic growth is rapid increase in population.[9] Dr. Ambedkar, as early as 1936, had pointed out this fact and insisted on the Assembly floor as well as public platforms to take suitable measures to arrest population growth to the develop the economy of the country.[10]

According to Dr. Ambedkar, there is a relation between poverty and increasing population. Over-population is the major cause of poverty in India. If Government does not take programmes for birth control, it would be very difficult to remove poverty. Suppose Government has taken programmes for the eradication poverty, but there are no measures for birth control; in this situation, the population would increase and poverty would remain as it was. Now there are many studies regarding population and poverty. These studies show that unless there is control on population, all the efforts of poverty eradication would be useless. Hence, it is the need of time to control birth rate.

M. Walter, in his book, 'Population and Poverty' (2004) writes that we now have solid evidence, based on new research, that work towards population goals help to reduce poverty at both household and national levels. At the national level, it is becoming increasingly clear that slower population growth encourages overall economic growth. Evidence also suggests that successful emerging economics almost always have favourable demographics.[11] Now we know that Dr. Ambedkar's views regarding the relation between poverty and population are true, which were expressed about70 years ago.

Dr. Ambedkar's Resolution regarding Measures for Birth Control

Dr. Ambedkar was thinking on the burning problems, like poverty and pressure of population since 1918. He referred to the problem of increasing population and poverty in the election manifesto of his Independent Labour party in 1936. Dr. Ambedkar secured 14 seats out of 17 that his party contested in 1937 election of Bombay Assembly. During the period of Assembly, he used the forum of non-official resolution to invite attention of the party in power to some of the fundamental problems in the country. He was strong supporter of family planning. He also suggested measures for birth control, which are the only remedy to arrest the rising population

Dr. Ambedkar was well aware of the fact that the conservative religious society was against his ideas with tooth and nails. However, he dared to move a resolution regarding the measures for birth control in Bombay Legislative Assembly on 10 November 1938.

Though the resolution was moved by Prabhakar Janardhan Roham, M.L.A., Independent Labour Party and the speech appeared in his name, it is virtually the speech prepared by Dr. B.R. Ambedkar. Roham himself had candidly and honestly told this fact to M.P. Mangudkar, when Smt. Shantabai Dani, President of Maharashtra Branch of All India Republican Party was also present.[12] Roham said in these worlds, "Whatever views I have expressed in the house were the views of Dr. Babasaheb Ambedkar."

Prabhakar Roham said, "I feel myself highly glorified to reveal that Dr. Babasaheb Ambedkar encouraged me to put forth this non-official resolution on behalf of my party. In fact, I look upon Dr. Ambedkar as my 'Jnyaneshwar'—the God of knowledge under whose influence, I could chant the 'Vedas' of these thoughts."[13]

The Government of Maharashtra has published Dr. Babasaheb Ambedkar's writing and speeches. In the Part I of Vol. 2 of Dr. Ambedkar's writing and speeches, the speeches, which were delivered by him in the Bombay legislature, are published. Regarding the resolution on measures for birth control; the editor has given the following special note: "Speech delivered by Mr. P. J. Roham. He has expressly stated that the speech was based in all respects on the points drawn by Dr. Ambedkar for his own speech and that Dr. Ambedkar is the father of this speech. Mr. Roham further states that he was complimented by Dr. Ambedkar for almost reproducing the speech, which he had contemplated to deliver in the Assembly, but he could not do so owing to his inability to attend the Assembly on that day, i.e., on 10 November 1938."[14] It is obviously clear that the same speech was prepared by Dr. Ambedkar himself.

It must be remembered that this non-official resolution was officially moved by the Independent Labour Party of which Dr. Ambedkar was the founder and leader. He used to hold regular meeting of the legislative wing of the party. He used to provide all possible arguments for the discussion in the House to the members of his party. He sometimes dictated almost the entire speech for the members of the legislative party of Independent Labour Party. The speech on birth-control was one amongst such speeches.[15] The most important thing is that Dr. Ambedkar had himself referred to the problem of population in the election manifesto of his Independent Labour Party in the interview, which was published in *The Times of India*, dated 15 August 1936. Hence, there is no doubt that the views of the Independent Labour Party were the views of Dr. Ambedkar. Roham himself cleared the fact.

According to Dr. Ambedkar, "very few have an adequate idea of the immense loss sustained by children born of persons, who are handicapped either physically, mentally or financially. The parents as well as the society also stuffier very much. The prevention of the births of such children would considerably reduce the death-rate among mothers, who succumb to childbirth and its concomitant disease. Lower infantile mortality would improve public health by removing the many diseases due to want of even the prime necessities of life felt by many persons, check the offences perpetrated by persons suffering from intense poverty and would bring about an all round uplift of society by affording full scope to its spiritual advancement."[16]

Dr. Ambedkar said that the present keen struggle of life renders timely marriage impossible for many and, thus, exposes them to various diseases and habits. Many women become invalids for life and some even lose their lives by the birth of children in their diseased condition or in great numbers or in too rapid succession. Attempts at abortion, resorted to for the prevention of unwanted progeny, exact a heavy toll of female lives. Unwanted children are often neglected by their mothers and, hence, they become nothing, but a burden to society, which is further deteriorated by the addition of defective progeny from diseased persons.[17]

Dr. Ambedkar argued that birth-control is the only sovereign method that can do away with all these calamities. Whenever a woman is disinclined to bear a child for any reason whatsoever, she must be in a position to prevent conception and bringing forth progeny should be entirely dependent on the choice of women. Society would in no way profit by the addition of unwanted progeny. Only those children, who are welcomed by their parents, can be of social benefit and hence every woman must be enabled to resort to prevention of conception quite easily.[18]

Dr. Ambedkar pointed out that poverty is the root cause of immorality and birth-control is the 'sine qua non' for every progress; we must consider the means to attain that end.[19]

He suggested that to be satisfied with only that much of sexual enjoyment that is necessary for getting the desired number of children and to banish sexual thought from one's mind when progeny is not required is one of the ways. The use of modern contraceptives is the other way. As for the first way, it must be remembered that while continence in the unmarried state may be possible, it is nothing but displaying ignorance about human nature to expect that young and healthy married couples living together and fond of each other, can observe continence for years together. The cases of strong-willed persons, whose minds are not affected in the presence of objects of enjoyment apart, there is no doubt that human beings are bound to fall prey to influence of enticements. It is not strange, therefore, that this fact, which is as clear as daylight, is denied by some.[20]

Dr. Ambedkar cleared that self-control has been proved to be absolutely useless for birth-control from the experience of several centuries and ages. Even the advocates of continence cannot claim that ordinary persons will be able to eschew sexual intercourse throughout their lives. The laying aside of continence even for a single day in a year may lead to an annual conception. Even if we assume that self-control enables certain persons to bring about birth-control, we cannot draw the conclusion that others will be able to follow them. It is necessary to remember that just as appetite for food differs in the case of different persons, so sexual appetite also varies from person to person.[21]

It is wrong to hold that because the ideal of large families is still preferred in the society, nobody wishes to limit his family. Human beings, who earnestly desire to be saddled with large families, are rare. Ordinary persons do want to limit their families and do not even flinch to have recourse to diabolical methods, such as abortion, infanticide, etc. *The People's Tribune* in 1934, found that in 1933 over 24,000 dead bodies of little infants were picked up in the streets of Shanghai alone and the same state prevails throughout most of China. It is bitter and terrible poverty that makes the parents expose their infants.[22]

Dr. Ambedkar advocates that in the light of such instances, it is futile to hope that ordinary persons will be able to avoid progeny merely through self-control. It is, therefore, established that there is no way without recourse to modern contraceptives. To deny the necessity of those remedies is to show one's preference for abortions, infanticides, etc.[23]

Dr. Ambedkar said that some people think that they would be losers if the numbers in their particular race, religion or region were lessened. They are afraid that their adversaries would thereby be able to gain ground over them. In the first place, it is necessary to remember in this connection that the rate of increase of a population does not necessarily dwindle down as soon as family limitation is resorted to. That rate is dependent not merely on the birth-rate, but chiefly on the survival rate. The experience of several scientists from different places has proved that the higher the birth rate, the higher is the death rate also and no sooner the birth rate goes down, the death rate also declines. The result is that not only is the survival rate not adversely affected, but very often it even rises. Dr. Marie Stopes has found from the experience gained in 'The Mother's Clinic' that the greater the number of conceptions, the higher is the rate of maternal and infantile mortality. Similar is the experience of other scientists.[24]

According to Dr. Ambedkar, due to the excessive child mortality, the rate of growth of the population of countries like India is not equal to that of countries like England, though the birth rates in countries of the former type are higher than those in the latter type. The birth rates of England are nearly half of that of India. Yet we find that the population in England increased by nearly 23 per cent between 1901 and 1931, while the population in India rose only 127 per cent in the same period. This will show that even for a rapid growth of numbers, the better way is to adopt the practice of birth-control and, thus, cut down infantile mortality.[25] In the world, we can witness many societies that are small in numbers, but distinguished in respect of wealth, culture, etc. In our country, the Parasi community is an illustration of this point. To hanker after quantity is, therefore, not a very profitable ideal.[26]

Dr. Ambedkar was in favour of contraception. Contraception is an important measure of birth control. Therefore, he gave the example of Western countries. Through this example of Western countries, he cleared that modern contraception is utilised by persons of all races, religions and strata. For instance, it is found that the notion that the

Roman Catholics are against birth-control is unfounded. France is a Roman Catholic country and still it is notorious that the birth-rate in the country is quite low.

India's birth rate was 46.4 per cent in 1931, whereas Western countries' birth rate was below 18 per cent. For the support of our statement, Dr. Ambedkar gave the birth rate of Western countries in the resolution.[27]

The following ten countries had the lowest birth rate in 1932.[28]

Sweden	14.5
Germany	15.1
Austria	15.2
England and Wales	15.3
Norway	16.3
Australia	16.4
Switzerland	16.7
New Zealand	17.1
United States	17.3
France	17.3

The following figures, the birth rates of important cities, illustrate the very point. They are all for 1927 or 1928.[29]

London	16.1
Cologne	16.0
Genoa	14.6
Milan	14.5
Turin	13.2
Prague	12.5
Munich	12.0
Vienna	10.6

Dr. Ambedkar cleared that among the three countries with the lowest birth rate are Austria, which is entirely Catholic and Germany, which is one third Catholic. With the exception of London, all the above cities are solidly Roman Catholic, yet they all have a lower birth rate than London. Three of them are in Mussolini's Italy. Again, he cleared that it will be thus seen that the fear that other communities will neglect birth control and will become stronger in numbers, is altogether a baseless argument.[30]

Dr. Ambedkar pointed out the reason of modern wars. According to him, speeches of statesman, who are responsible for wars, clearly show that economic difficulties due to pressure of population are at the root of most of the modern wars. Bernhardi, the Kaiser Hitler, Mussolini and Goering have often stressed this point in no ambiguous words.[31] For instance, Adolf Hitler says in his book, Mein Kampf, "Through the man multiplication of the German people before the war, the question of providing the necessary daily bread came in an ever sharper manner into the fore-ground of all political and economic thought and action.

Further, he says, "Only an adequate amount of room upon this party secures to a nation the freedom of its existence. The National Socialist movement must endeavour to do away with the disproportion between our numbers and our territory. Ground and territory must be the object of our foreign politics."(pp. 728-35)

In his historic speech, delivered on the 12 September 1938, Hitler says, "They expect Germany, where 140 persons are squeezed into a square kilometre to keep her Jews, whereas the powers with only a few persons per kilometre do not want them."

Similarly, Mussolini said, "We are hungry for land because we are prolific and intend to remain so" (from "Foreign Affairs," October, 1926). "Italy demands that her indisputable need of sun and land shall be recognised by all other nations. Should they fail to do so, Italy will be forced to take matters into her own hand." (From *Sunday Times*, 14 November 1926)

Dr. Ambedkar argued that it was, therefore, obvious that all those who stand for permanent world brotherhood, must discountenance every attempt at increase of numbers and must try their best to limit populations by means of birth control.[32]

Dr. Ambedkar said that the fear that birth control propaganda will fail to filter down to the messes and the result of the movement will thus be dysgenic instead of eugenic, is also groundless.[33] Further, he said, "The experience gained in Western countries establishes the fact that the lower classes do take advantage of contraceptives as soon as they are made cognizant of them, the need being greater in their cases. He expressed profound faith in the wisdom of the poor masses. It was said that the masses in the rural areas are illiterate and ignorant and, therefore, they would not be able to follow birth control intelligently. He said that the masses in our country, though illiterate, are intelligent enough to know in what their own interest lies and, hence, there is no doubt that they will fully utilise this invention also as soon as they are made aware of its existence. Vasectomy would be found to be useful in the case of such persons and, hence, the Government and Municipalities must provide facilities in this respect in their hospitals.

Emigration is not a remedy to reduce population. Therefore, Dr. Ambedkar said that emigration is sometimes suggested as a remedy for finding an outlet to over population, but that remedy also is not very promising. Compulsion in emigration amounting to transportation is out of question. Very few persons have the courage and the inclination necessary for leaving one's own country endeared to one's heart by reminiscences of childhood and the presence of relatives and friends and made agreeable by a suitable climate being found to be an unsuitable one and in which the inhabitants are different from oneself in language, customs and manners. Besides this, it must be kept in mind that sparsely population countries are unwilling to accommodate others because they require elbow room for their own increasing progeny. Canada is a colony in the British Empire inhabited by Englishmen, but it is notorious that the Canadians refused to allow English labourers, who had gone there for seasonal work; to settle in their land.[34]

Dr. Ambedkar argued that one more point in this connection is also worth mentioning. Emigration cannot solve the population problem of a country permanently. Like air, expanding population has a tendency to fill up the vacuum immediately, leading to the recurrence of the former condition and hence it is obvious that there is no way without birth control.[35]

According to Dr. Ambedkar, late marriage is not the solution to reduce population. He said that some think that as soon as child marriages are given up and late marriage one introduced, the increase in population will be checked. But this belief is also an unfounded one. In the first place, years must elapse before the age at which girls are married would be sufficiently raised in our country. The years of greatest fertility in the case of girls are those between 18 to 22. In Western countries, women marry after this period. That is, they marry when their time of greatest fertility is over. When we notice the difficulties in the enforcement of the Sharada Act, fixing the minimum age of marriage of girls at 14, we can easily see that it is almost useless to hope that in the near future women in our country will postpone their marriages up to 22 and population will be checked thereby.[36]

For supporting his above statement, Dr. Ambedkar gave reference of P. K. Wattal's conclusions regarding fertility.[37] Mr. Wattal has drawn the following conclusions from the fertility enquiry conducted specially in connection with the 1931 Census.

1. The girls married at ages below twenty give birth to a smaller number of children than girls married at ages above twenty.
2. The survival rate of children born to mothers married at ages below twenty is much less than that of children born to mothers married at ages above twenty.

Therefore, Dr. Ambedkar argued that these conclusions show us that even when late marriages world come into vogue, generally, there is no chance of population being appreciably checked by. More children would live up to mature ages and, hence, there is a chance of an increase and not a decrease in the rate of growth of our population.[38]

Dr. Ambedkar had also given reference of sociologist, Dr. G.S. Ghurye in his speech. Dr. Ghurye in his article, "Fertility of the Indian Census of 1931" (*Journal of the University of Bombay*, Vol. III, May 1934) says, "if the above tentative conclusion about the correlation between fertility and the age of woman at marriage should prove to be correct, then with the increase in woman's age at marriage, which is quite essential, there would be an increase in the fertility of women. As it is, I believe, our population is very large and our increase undesirable and to help its increase at a greater rate would be suicidal. With our efforts to raise the woman's age at marriage, therefore, there must also be carried on an intensive campaign for control of birth".

Dr. Ambedkar gave warning that if the people are unable to marry at proper ages, then prostitution will be encouraged and other evil consequences will also follow.

According to Dr. Ambedkar, economic freedom of woman is not helpful to reduce the population growth. He said that the view is held that economic independence of woman will lessen the growth of population, but it also does not hold water. Economic independence has no power to free a person from the clutches of Eros. Few women can observe perfect continence throughout their lives and, hence, this remedy would be fruitless. Even now, women of the lower classes are actually helping their families with their own earnings, but that fact does not seem to help family limitation to any extent.[39]

Dr. Ambedkar said that some persons hold the view that though birth control may be necessary on medical and hygienic grounds, still it is not required for solving economic difficulties. They maintain that our country has got much scope for economic and agricultural development and efforts in those directions would raise the standard of our people appreciably. According to him, after close examination, however, this view also is found to be quite untenable.[40]

Further, he said that want of sufficient capital and rich customers would prevent any material development of our industries. Similarly, insufficiency of fertile lands, rainfall and manures stand in the way of any substantial increase in our agricultural production. In our province, 86.4 per cent of the cultivable land has already been brought under the plough and it is doubtful whether even a fraction of the rest of the land is of any value. According to the Report of the Royal Commission on Indian Agriculture, much of such land is worthless. A great portion of agricultural land in our country has become barren through incessant cropping and want of sufficient manures. Through the excessive growth of population, our country will suffer from deficiency of forests and pasture land.[41]

Dr. Ambedkar said that although it may be admitted that self-rule may affect some betterment of the lot of our masses, no lasting and appreciable improvement in the economic condition of our people could be hoped for unless the growth of our population is deliberately checked. As has been already explained with every opportunity that afforded its expansion, population begins to grow rapidly and thus nullifies all the advantages secured through great efforts. Hence, experience had made scientists to hold the view that unless precaution is taken to regulate population growth by means of birth control along with efforts to improve the economic condition of the people, there cannot be any substantial and permanent rise in the standard of living of the masses.[42]

Dr. Ambedkar held that the fact that more self rule is powerless to effect an all round improvement in the condition of people is demonstrated to the hilt by the examples of many independent nations. Although through various, including a low birth rate, the economic condition of the inhabitants of countries like England and America is superior to that obtaining in our country—poverty prevents many of our countrymen from obtaining nourishing food, still it is far from satisfactory.[43] He said that even there, many find it difficult to maintain a standard of life necessary for perfect health. According to President

Roosevelt, One-third of the inhabitants of America do not get sufficient nourishing food. One of the reasons for this is that even their birth control is not practiced to the extent to which it is necessary. There is plenty of fertile land per head in countries that are newly settled and, hence, the people there get more nourishing food than what is obtained by persons in thickly population nations.

For supporting his view, Dr. Ambedkar gave following figures of consumption per head per annum in Australia and Italy.

Food Consumption

Food	*Australia*	*Italy*
Milk and its Products (Gals)	102	23
Meat (1bs.)	202	35
Fruit (1bs.)	104	40
Sugar (1bs.)	107	18
Wheat (1bs.)	207	351

Every Article of food except wheat is consumed in far greater quantities in Australia than in Italy. Out of the nations of the old world, countries like Holland that have their birth rates much lower through birth control are much happier than the rest. In the Bombay Presidency, the amount of milk available per head per day is only one quarter in totals. According to authorities on nutrition, every individual must get on an average at least one pint of milk per day.

Dr. Ambedkar held that the main object of the movement for birth control is to bring about a state of things wherein every country will have its birth rate suitably reduced, so that it would thus be able to maintain its population decently with the aid of its own produce.[44]

Dr. Ambedkar said that some are under the impression that modern scientific discoveries have solved the problem of food for mankind and that it is only mis-distribution that is at the root of the present economic difficulties. Fair distribution of property would, in their opinion, bring about plenty everywhere. There is no doubt that in many places injustice prevails in the division of property and every impartial public worker must take all steps to secure justice for wronged persons in this respect.[45] In the opinion of Dr. Ambedkar, it is, however, necessary to remember that more equal distribution will never be able to bring about a permanent and material amelioration of the condition of the masses unless growth of population is controlled by means of family limitation.

Dr. Ambedkar warned that the efforts of the present Congress Government to uplift the masses of Bombay presidency will go in vain if the population problem is not tackled by means of birth control.[46]

Dr. Ambedkar concluded his speech in a very effective way. He appealed not only to reason, but to the noble feeling in men. He said in his concluding speech, "Bombay is the gateway of India and his movement also entered this country through that very gate. It would be in the fitness of things, therefore, that it should also be nurtured in this very province. Few people get an opportunity for doing acts that would immortalise their names. Birth control movement has afforded such an opportunity to our provincial Government and it is hoped that they will not let it slip, but will fully utilise it for the benefit of themselves and the people.[47]

Opposition to Resolution

After the end of the speech of Dr. Ambedkar, T.S. Jadhao, MLA stood up and opposed the resolution regarding measures for birth control and said, "It is a pity that honourable members should try to import western ideas and methods into our country. I do not think that artificial birth control is the only method for controlling population. It is much better to bring about changes in diet and other habits of life in order to achieve the object in view than to adopt the measures recommended by westerners. Self control is the best remedy, and the avoidance of stimulating food and drink, which increase sexual appetite, helps a man to have self control. It is said that the Government should afford facilities for propaganda of birth control. Example is better than precept. The measures recommended by Mahatma Gandhi should be adopted.[48]

Further, he said that propaganda is not needed. Self control is all that is necessary. Instead of depending on all sorts of appliances for birth control, it is better to have self control. Mahatma Gandhi laid down the rules.

The legislative party in the Bombay Assembly was committed to Gandhian philosophy and, therefore, most of the members of the Congress party in the Assembly were against the measures for birth control.

The followers of Gandhian philosophy put forward a number of arguments to oppose the measures for birth control. Mr. Morarji Desai, who was the Revenue Minister, said, "What I want to argue all the while is that people should have self control. I know self control is a very difficult thing. In this matter, we do not expect that everybody will reach that high stage of Brahmacharya, which Mahatma Gandhi expects for himself and for others. But, in the matter of preventing the evil to women, that stage of Brahmacharya is certainly not necessary. What self control is necessary for man is that he should not approach his wife, that he should remain away, that he should have a self control over himself. It is just possible that he may have impulses in his own body periodically, and if he loses the vital fluid at times, it will not be an evil as far as the woman is concerned; and even as far as he is concerned that will not deteriorate his health. I have no doubt that this sort of self control is not impossible for people. I cannot understand why that should be impossible.[49]

Dr. M.D.D. Gilder, who was the Minister for Public Health, also opposed this resolution by advancing a number of arguments. One of his interesting arguments was that our national income is increasing faster than the population. The question of increase in poverty, therefore, is irrelevant.

For example, he said in his speech, "Now just make a comparative study. As I said, the figure of population is 117 now for 100 in 1900. The index figure of production as worked out by Professor Karve is 157. As worked out by other economic experts, it is 144. Corrected and adjusted to the level of prices, it worked out at 130, so that at the present moment, in the last 30 years, the production has certainly gone ahead of the population. One thing is certain that the population has not grown and is not growing faster than production.[50]

There were some other pseudo scientific or irrational arguments put forth in the course of debate. Gandhian approach followed by those people was not dogmatic and rigid, but was very fanatical. The Gandhians were, therefore, very much against Dr. Ambedkar's resolution regarding the measures for birth control.

The next group in the Assembly was that of Marxists, Communists and Socialists. Communism also opposed the measures of birth control not only in India, but all over the world.[51] Karl Marx himself criticised the Malthusian theory of population. The major contention of Marxist philosophy is that capitalism is mainly responsible for the poverty of the masses and in order to divert the attention on the poor masses from the main cause, the capitalists deliberately propound such theories and try to perpetuate the life of capitalism in the world.

Therefore, the communists and socialist in India followed the same argument and opposed the concept of birth control. Capitalism might be one of the causes of poverty of the masses, but the position taken by the Marxists in those days was that it was the only cause for poverty. As soon as we change the ownership of the means of production, the problem of poverty would be automatically solved. The Marxists, because of their doctrinaire approach to the problem, not only opposed the resolution, but tried to ridicule the whole issue.

The third group in the Assembly was mainly the group of communalists, like the Hindu Mahasabha, the Muslim League, etc. The philosophy of Hindu nationalism was also against the measures of birth control.[52] They had faith in aggressive and expansionist communalism and, therefore, they were interested in increasing the population of the country.

In the thirties, there was the rise of Hitler and Mussolini in Germany and Italy and some of the legislative members of this period were influenced by the fascist philosophy of those leaders.

The Muslim League opposed it mainly on religious ground. For example, Ali Bahadur Khan said in his speech, "The Christians opposed it because they do not want any interference in the so called work of God, as he put it. And the Hindus have their own solution. But the Mohammadans have a solution, which is just the opposite of both these. There, the problem has been talked in a very aggressive fashion, the contention being that population must increase. The views of the prophet on this are—and I might quote his own Arabic words first, "Oh people, you have to produce children and increase population." This is a literal translation of the saying of the prophet. But, then, the question of production has not been left out of consideration. The solution is there is sufficient food on the surface of the earth; you expand, go about and travel about and you will find that this earth will give you sufficient to live upon. Therefore, both the problems are trickled in a particular fashion.[53]

The other religious minorities like Christians also on those days opposed the resolution on religious ground. Jamanadas M. Mehta, MLA, very ably summarised the major argument of these religious groups. He said, "First of all, we are best with prejudice against interfering with the work of God."

The theory is that marriages are made in Heaven and, therefore, girls and boys are produced in Heaven first and then they are sent down, and any attempt to limit population is an interference with the laws of nature, with religion and particularly our friends of the Roman Catholic persuasion are honestly convinced that birth control is sinful. Then, there is a certain prejudice due to tradition.[54]

Besides Gandhians, Marxists, Champions of Hindu Nationalism, Muslim League, Christians and other nationalist were also opposed to the resolution. Their central theme was that British Imperialism is responsible for the poverty and other consequential evil effects in the country. If the British Imperialism is liquidated, almost all the problems of our country would be automatically[55] solved.[56] So, it is futile to discuss the measures of birth control. There were a large number of nationalists, who subscribed to this thinking.

As a result of this, Dr. Ambedkar was probably the only political leader in India, who thought of this problem very seriously and analysed the issue in a very rational, scientific and pragmatic way. In the context of all India situation in those days, Dr. Ambedkar's thinking is not only very striking, but it also places him far ahead of his contemporaries.

Support Speeches for Resolution

Dr. Ambedkar's approach was more impressive in the context of the situation in the forties in India. Minority communities like the Scheduled Castes were getting reservation on the basis of their number, in the services as well as in the legislatures and other elected bodies. Limiting their population was apparently going against the interests of the Scheduled Castes. But Dr. Ambedkar convinced his followers that birth-control was primarily in the interest of the poor people like the Untouchables and other groups. He argued brilliantly on this issue. He raised a very pertinent question in this regard, namely, what is more important- birth rate or survival rate? Then, he argued that if there is a higher birth rate after three children, there is a higher mortality rate and poor survival rate. He, therefore, said that survival rate is more important than the birth-rate and control would go a long way in improving the health and financial condition of the Scheduled Caste people. This argument is not only convincing, but it is almost a profound truth that is universally applicable to all poor communities in the world.

B.K. Gaikawad, MLA of Independent Labour Party, supported the resolution moved by Dr. Ambedkar. He said in his speech, "The matter for consideration is whether there is enough food for all in this country and if there is, do the poor people get enough for themselves? On the one hand, we find in every Census report the population of our province increasing. On the other hand, we very well see that the unemployment in the province is increasing day by day. It is the bounden duty of the State to find out a better remedy to remove unemployment. To our mind, as there is no other remedy found out by the present Government, the birth control scheme may be accepted by them. This will go a long way to mitigate the poverty of our province. It is not honest to say that there is no unemployment. We very clearly see that several people are not in a position to get even bread twice a day. They lead their lives in a very miserable state. Many of them are going from door to door to beg; many young men and women go on applying to authorities of various departments to get a job to keep their body and soul tougher. Many of them have committed suicide, as they were not in a position to maintain themselves and their families. In my opinion, birth-control means nothing, but a check on the increase of unemployment and better nutrition of a limited family unit."[57]

Gaikawad has also invited attention to one of the important issues in this context. He said that there are certain communities, like Christians, Muslims and others, who are against the measures of birth-control. But, the resolution under discussion did not come in the way of those, who want increase in the population. But, let those, who do not want it, be given the facilities proposed in the resolution. He said that the only obligation on Government is to render financial assistance to institutions, which carry on propaganda and education in the use of birth-control methods. He later on said that, after all, is it not the removal of poverty by this indirect method? What about those, who find it impossible to bring up children by feeding and clothing them? There have been instances where children have been given up as human sacrifice simply out of despair.[58] He, therefore, said that let the Government offer facilities of birth-control to those people, who like to benefit from them. Why deprive those people, who have faith in this method only because a few sections of society oppose it on one ground or the other? This argument of Gaikawad was really very pragmatic and convincing at that time.

R.R. Bhole, MLA of Independent Labour Party, also gave speech to support the resolution. He said in his speech that they were of the opinion that birth-control would go a great way towards annihilating poverty.[59]

He has also drawn the attention of the House in this connection to a book called "*An Essay on the Principle of Population*". He said that the book would remove the misconception, which existed in this House that production increases far beyond the proportionate increase of population. But this argument was disapproved by various authorities, one of whom was Professor D.G. Karve. Originally, only principal crops were estimated; now all crops are estimated; hence, it appears to most readers that the production has increased in a greater proportion. But that is not the case.

He argued that the present condition of India is such that the people are poverty-stricken, and the only way in which we could diminish their property is by limiting the family units that exist today.[60] He further said that India today does not want quantity; India today wants quality. It is poverty, which makes them physical wrecks.

At the end of the speech, he said strongly that if they had at heart the good of the masses and if they were able to "deliver the goods" as they always say, they must adopt the resolution.[61]

After two days discussions on the resolution, the Deputy Speaker of Bombay Assembly put the resolution up for voting. It is interesting to know that when the resolution was put to voting, ten members, who supported it, were mainly from the Independent Labour Party and other 49 members opposed it. Thus, Dr. Ambedkar's historical resolution regarding measures for birth-control was negative.

Other Speeches of Dr. Ambedkar on Birth Control

The Untouchable Students' Conference was held in Bombay on 12 December 1938. Dr. Ambedkar advised students from the president's chair.[62] It is very interesting that one-fourth speech is related with the problem of population and birth control. Though the resolution regarding measures for birth-control was negative in the Legislative Assembly a month before. However, he did not leave that subject and he convinced the students why there must be limited family.

Dr. Ambedkar said in his speech that most of the students may be unmarried while several might have got married. But what were they going to do after marriage? A heavy responsibility rested on their shoulders in this respect. He said that he would illustrate the case of his father instead of theirs. He had fourteen children in all and amongst these, he was a student in the Elphinston College? He had to go barefooted and he used to put on a shirt of rough cloth and a torn coat of his father. On entering this college, they would find a photograph of Muller Sahib, who provided him with shirts for the last two years. He used to ponder how nice it would have been if his father had only four children instead of fourteen! It was his father and only he, who was responsible for his misery.

Further, he said that once, while going to the college, he forgot the railway-pass at home and on the same day, passes were checked. The ticket collector stopped him. But, he had not a single paisa with him and had to wait at the Church Gate station up to 4 p.m. Afterwards, his classmate named Kaikini came there and asked him why he was sitting there. When Ambedkar narrated to him what had happened, he paid four annas and relieved him from the place. His friend bought a ticket for him and sent him home. Thus, he blamed his father in this regard, as he did not understand his responsibility. Ambedkar did not feel it to be improper to point out this to his father, when he was wrong. He said that now, this responsibility rested on the students, as well as on women. They should see that what he spoke was meant not only for males, but also for females. After completing their studies, they would enter into service, but Ambedkar believed that most of them would become clerks and earn about ₹ 50 or ₹ 60 per month. And with this pay, if they had 14 children, what would happen to them? Would they set this responsibility on the society? He asked the students to consider deeply about this in their mind.

He further added that he is sure that they would not be ready to become *Sanyasis* and if somebody became one, it would be very nice! (Loud cheers). He said, "Don't laugh, as this is a very serious and important thing. I had five children out of which four expired. Now I don't feel sorry for this. On the other hand, I am happy. Had these children remained alive, it would have been greatly troublesome to carry the burden of their food and education. Now I have got only one son and I have to shoulder his responsibility. If you show 100th part of this responsibility for your children, it would be well and good. This is a matter of Social Welfare. If you produce five or six children, how will you afford to give them education and other facilities? I think, it would be in descending order, instead of ascending one. So, you must consider that leading a life like a brute is against humanity."

Dr. Ambedkar focused on the problem of more children through his personal experience. He advised the students, not to produce more children. If they produced more children then it would be very difficult to carry the burden of their food and education. He gave the example of his father, who had fourteen children. He didn't hesitate to blame his own father for his (Dr. Ambedkar's) misery. Through the example of his own life, he gave warning to the students regarding producing more children.

Dr. Ambedkar had great regard and respect for women. Through his writing and speeches, he always held them in high esteem and gave them all due importance. He always held that for the all round development of the society, women are equally responsible. Therefore, he always used to advise them.

The All India Depressed Classes Conference was held at Nagpur on 18-19 July, 1942. All India Depressed Women's Conference was also held on 20 July 1942 at the same place. This conference was attended by 20 to 25 thousand women. In this conference, Dr. Ambedkar said that the development of women is the measure of a certain society's development. He added, "You have attended this conference in a large number; which itself proves that our society is now certainly on the path of progress; there is no doubt about it."[63]

While advising woman as to how they should live and what they should do, Dr. Ambedkar said, "Learn to live clean and be free from all evils. Educate your children and encourage ambitions in their mind. Put in their mind that they will become great. Remove sense of diffidence from their mind. Do not haste to get married. Marriage means responsibility. Unless they become able to perform economic responsibility, do not insist upon them to get married. The one who gets married, they should keep in mind that producing more children is a bad act. Though we do not get facilities in our childhood, but it is the duty of parents to give good education and better upbringing for every child. Most important thing is that every married girl should give co-operation in every activities of her husband as a friend. I hope that if you follow this advice then all of you will get respect and success and the depressed classes also will get respect and success."

Ambedkar strongly opposed producing more children. According to him, producing more children is a bad act. He believed that small family is the key of happiness. Parents can give good education and better upbringing for their children only when they have small families. Hence, he advised the people not to produce more children, not to haste to get married. Birth-control is the only way to keep small size of family. That is why he moved resolution regarding measures for birth-control.

ENDNOTES

1. Kasare, Dr. M. L. (1996), *Economic Philosophy of B. R. Ambedkar*, B. I. Publications Pvt. Ltd. Delhi, p. 258.
2. *Dr. Babasaheb Ambedkar Writing and Speeches*, Vol. 1, Education Department, Government of Maharashtra, Mumbai, 1979, p. 473.
3. *Ibid*, p. 474.
4. *Dr. Babasaheb Ambedkar Writing and Speeches*, Vol. 17, Part-Two, Dr. Babasaheb Ambedkar Source Material Publication Committee, Higher Education Department, Government of Maharashtra, Mumbai, 2003, p. 415.
5. *Ibid*, p. 416.
6. *Ibid*, p. 416.
7. *Dr. Babasaheb Ambedkar Writing and Speeches*, Vol. 2, Education Department, Government of Maharashtra, Mumbai, 1982, p. 19.
8. *Ibid*, p. 19.
9. Kasare, Dr. M. L. *op. cit*, p. 257.
10. *Ibid*, p. 257.
11. Walter, M. (2004), *Population and Poverty*, Adhyayan Publishers and Distributors, Delhi, p. 3.
12. Mangudkar, M. P. (1976), *Dr. Ambedkar and Family Planning*, Publisher Mrs. Suvarne Mangudkar, Poona, p. 15.
13. *Ibid*, p. 19.
14. *Dr. Babasaheb Ambedkar Writing and Speeches*, Vol. 2, Part 1, p. 263.
15. *Ibid*, p. 15.
16. *Bombay Legislative Debates*, Vol. 4 (Part-57) 10 November 1938, p. 4025.
17. *Ibid*, p. 4025.
18. *Ibid*, p. 4025.
19. *Ibid*, p. 4025, 4026.
20. *Ibid*, p. 4026
21. *Ibid*, p. 4026
22. *Ibid*, p. 4028.
23. *Ibid*, p. 4028.
24. *Ibid*, p. 4028, 4029.
25. *Ibid*, p. 4029.
26. *Ibid*, p. 4029.
27. *Ibid*, p. 4029.
28. *Ibid*, p. 4029.
29. *Ibid*, p. 4030
30. *Ibid*, p. 4030.
31. *Ibid*, p. 4030.

32. *Ibid*, p. 4031.
33. *Ibid*, p. 4031.
34. *Ibid*, p. 4032, 4033.
35. *Ibid*, p. 4033.
36. *Ibid*, p. 4033.
37. *Ibid*, p. 4033.
38. *Ibid*, p. 4033.
39. *Ibid*, p. 4034.
40. *Ibid*, p. 4034.
41. *Ibid*, p. 4034.
42. *Ibid*, p. 4035.
43. *Ibid*, p. 4035.
44. *Ibid*, p. 4036.
45. *Ibid*, p. 4036.
46. *Ibid*, p. 4037.
47. *Ibid*, p. 4037.
48. *Ibid*, p. 4038.
49. *Bombay Legislative Debates*, Vol. 4 (Part 57) 11 November 1938, p. 4093.
50. *Ibid*, p. 4098.
51. Mangudkar, M. P. *op. cit*, p. 3.
52. *Ibid*, p. 4.
53. *Bombay Legislative Debates*, Vol. 4 (Part 57), p. 4082, 4083.
54. *Ibid*, p. 4069.
55. Mangudkar, M. P., *op. cit*, p. 5.
56. *Ibid*, p. 6.
57. *Bombay Legislative Debates*, Vol. 4 (Part 57), p. 4083, 4084.
58. *Ibid*, p. 4084, 4085, 4086.
59. *Ibid*, p. 4094.
60. *Ibid*, p. 4095.
61. *Ibid*, p. 4096.
62. *Dr. Babasaheb Ambedkar Writing and Speeches*, Vol. 18, Part 2, Dr. Ambedkar Source Material Publication Committee, Higher Education Department, Government of Maharashtra, Bombay, 2003 p. 237.
63. *Ibid*, p. 430.

4

Impact of Population Growth on Economic and Social Development

Today, mankind is facing many challenges. But the most significant and the most menacing is the problem of growing population. Rapidly growing population is the main problem in developing countries of Asia and Latin America. Every generation has had its own problems, but the ever increasing population may be viewed as the super-problem of the present generation.

Population growth, though it may directly affect some particular countries or regions of the world, at least indirectly affects the whole world. Considering the seriousness of the population problem, the General Assembly of the United Nations voted for and carried out a resolution in December 1962 recognising the intimate relationship that exists between the growth of population and economic development and suggested certain measures to be taken to face the problem on an emergency footing.

After the Second World War, the world witnessed unprecedented population growth, particularly in its less developed regions. This has aroused world-wide interest in the study of population dynamics and its impact on economic and social development. There is a growing awareness of the consequences of unabated population growth, which is likely to upset the balance between people and resources; between the hopes and aspirations of the people; and the opportunities available to them. Large populations and rapid rates of growth, found across most of the developing world, are recent phenomena.

Rapid population increase poses a serious threat to the development efforts of less developed countries. The problem of population is not merely quantitative, but also qualitative in nature, as the implication of population growth on the quality of life and the well-being of the people is great.

There is no doubt that human resource is the best resource that cannot be matched with any other resources in the world, but when this resource proves unproductive or less productive, then, it becomes a burden on the quality of life of other persons as well as on the development and prosperity of the nation. Unwanted increasing population is a hurdle in the way of economic and social development.

It is now widely recognised that population factors are not only important in their own right, but are also significant in influencing trends in social and economic progress, at both the global and national levels. The relevance of population factors in the developing countries has increased considerably during the last fifty years, mostly as a consequence of the onset of their demographic transition and their national efforts to faster social and economic development through development planning.

In 2001, India's population was 102.70 crores, which is increasing almost by two per cent each year. This population is much more than the geographical size of the nation in relation to other nations of the world. It is a matter of grave concern. Population growth has a bad impact on economic and social development of the nation. This is why population growth is a main obstacle in the economic and social development of the developing countries. India is an over-populated country. Many demographers have cleared in their studies that population growth influences very badly the economic and social progress of a country. Hence, the country cannot progress. While discussing the problem of population growth, it is necessary to understand the impact of population on the economic and social development.

Impact of Population Growth on Economic Development

The economic development of a country is closely related to the qualitative as well as quantitative structure of its population and vice-versa.

Economic development and population development are supplementary and complementary to each other and each affects directly or indirectly the other. The result of this relationship depends on the efficiency, merit and tendencies of the persons involved in it.

Manpower is the ends and means to both. Hence, the manpower planning or planning of human resource is a vital element in national development. Thus, man is both means and ends, which changes with the variables of economic development. Man influences the economic development as a means of production with the combination of other factors of production. He also boosts economy by being a consumer, who demands production as both consumer and producer of goods. Therefore, there is inter-relation between population and economic development.

Population growth can be both a stimulant as well as an obstacle to economic development. Albert Hirschman holds the view that population growth is stimulant to economic growth in the sense that when the number increases and causes a decline in the standard of living, there is general resistance by the communities against it and they try their best to control the environment and organise themselves for further development. Arthur Lewis explains that in a backward economy, population growth promotes overall development of the economy from the subsistence sector at a wage in the later sector. This view has been further extended by Jorgenson in his model of dual economy. The limits to the expansion of capitalist sector are set by the availability of cheap labour, which is inadequate in relation to the availability of capital and land, under a given technology, any increase in population will be considered beneficial.

J.R. Hicks looks at industrial revolution as a vast boom brought about by unprecedented rise in population. Bose rejects the pessimism of Malthus and Ricardo about agriculture's ability to feed growing population due to the law of diminishing returns. He asserts that the pressure of population on land has served as the principal inducement of technological innovations. Jullian Simon takes this argument further by emphasising that the ultimate resource is people, who exert their will and imagination for their own benefit and for the benefit of all of us. More people implies more ideas, more creative talents, more skills and thus better technology. In the long-run, population growth is not a problem, but an opportunity, which removes the constraints imposed by natural resources. Thus, population growth as a stimulant to economic development is perceived as a factor leading to enhanced supply of goods and services. Large population leading to more supply of labour force not only produces more with given level of technology, but also with improved technology. Human beings have a tremendous capacity to respond to crisis situation, particularly when it threatens to lower their living standards. In such situations, creative facilities, better talent and improved skills help in removing the constraints on the production process. Alvin Hansen developed the model of 'Frontier Sprit', in which he took two functions—demand function and investment function—to analyse the impact of a rapidly growing population on economic growth. The optimum population theory analyses the relationship between population and resources. Edwin Cannon defines optimum population as the population producing maximum output with existing levels of technology, knowledge and resources. According to him, there is a relationship between population and natural resources of a region. With an increase in population, production goes on increasing up to a maximum point after which it starts declining with no more increase in the population. Besides Cannon, there are many others, who have defined the concept of optimum population on the basis of economic welfare, real income, employment, and level of living.

Though some economists and writers explain that population growth is a stimulant to economic development. But, it is only one side of the population growth. Many empirical studies on population observed that population growth is not stimulant to economic development, but it is an obstacle to economic development.

Following are the adverse impact of population growth on economic development.

1. *Impact on Per Capita Income*

The rate of economic development is much affected by the rate of growth of population, size and composition of population and age-structure of the population. It is sheer arithmetic that suggests that with a given growth of national income, the increase in the rate of population affects unfavourably the rise in the per capita income. In certain circumstances, there can be an actual reduction in the per capita income. As Enke has put it, if the rate of technological innovation cannot be forced, and is not advanced by faster population-growth, a rapid proportionate growth in population can cause an actual reduction in income per capita. The per capita national income of a country may increase either by reduction in population number, emigration, higher mortality rate or by increase in the national income. Thus, the demographic characteristics affect directly or indirectly, the economic development of a country.

The per capita income of a country has a direct relationship with its population size. If population growth is constant, the per capita income will increase with increase in total income. On the other hand, per capita income decreases, if the rate of increase of total national income becomes lesser than the rate of population growth. If both population and national income are increasing at the same rate, the per capita income will remain constant. At the same time, the total production and national income depends on the nature, efficiency, age and sex-structure and technical know-how of its working population.

The standard of living of the people is mostly influenced by the increase in population. If growth rate of population is greater than the rate of investments, then the standard of living of the people will deteriorate because of low per capita national income, and thus, there will be great necessity of human investment. Human investment is that investment, which is required for the maintenance of a standard of living with increase in population. Whereas, economic investment is that investment which is required for maintaining a higher rate of increase in the national income to enable to have better standard of living by increasing the per capita income.

Hence, human investment is determined by population growth; whereas economic investment is related with desired per capita income in spite of population growth. An intensive investment (where no increase of population and the additional capital on capital formed utilised for the people) increases the per capita national income apart from increasing total income of the country. But, an extensive-investment (where for the increased population the additional capital issued) increases the total national income keeping the per capita income constant.

Hence, faster growth rate of population affects adversely the per capita national income in the above two ways. Every increase in population decreases the per capita national income.

The economic development of a country depends on its working population, which is the total of men and women in the age-group of 15-64 years. This working population depends on the fertility and mortality rates of the country. High birth rate retards the economic development of a country, because it increases the burden of dependency on the working population, so reduces the amount of investment.

2. *Impact on Capital Formation*

A high rate of capital formation is very important for the development of any country. But, the fast growing population makes it difficult to achieve this objective. It, in fact, reduces resources for capital formation. This it does in the following two ways.

(i) *Eats away Investment Resources*: The investment resources used for maintaining the present low level of per capita income of the rising population is a minus item, which reduces the total resources of capital formation called "demographic investment". It is just to sustain the additional population at that income. The amount involved is quite sizable. An illustration is given to explain the point.

As investment depends on the capital output ratio, one may make a realistic assumption of this ratio at 4:1. This means that for the production of one unit of output, four units of capital are required. Assume also that the population is rising at the rate of 2.5 per cent. To enable the additional population to maintain the same per capita income, it would be necessary to make investment of the order of as much as ten per cent (4 × 2.5).

Economist George C. Zaidan has estimated that for countries like India, Columbia, etc. Ten per cent capital accumulation is essential to keep the per capita income at the same level.

Over and above this demographic investment, there is the "economic investment" for raising the per capita income. How much additional investment is required for this purpose depends upon the objective. If one is to take the objective of say five per cent rise in per capita income, then the resources needed for the economic investment will be 20 per cent.

Thus, to bring about an increase of five per cent in per capita income, an investment of 30 per cent (10% for demographic investment and 20% for economic development) will be required. Considering that no country has ever achieved this rate for long, this is impossible.

Thus, with lower population growth, the economic investment becomes feasible and high growth a practical proposition. In other words, with high population growth, capital formation to raise growth rate becomes a very difficult task.

(ii) *Lower Saving*: Fast population growth also adversely affects saving and, therefore, capital formation. This happens because of the rise in consumption that rapidly growing population involves. The additions to population means additions to the large number of existing consumers. The newborns, till they reach the working age, are just so many more mouths to feed. With an increase in the number of consumers, even if the per capita expenditure remains the same, the total consumption will rise. Given the level of income, an increase in consumption means less saving.

The consumption need are both for the private goods, services (like food, clothing, shelter, etc.) involving private expenditure, and for public goods (like drinking water, educational and medical facilities, transport, etc.) requiring government spending.

In this connection, one may suggest that the way out of this problem is the use of foreign savings. There is no doubt that foreign capital does play and has played an important part in the development of underdeveloped countries like India, at least in the initial stages of development. But it must be remembered that foreign capital is not available just for the asking, to any extent and on really soft terms. Generally, it has many and often stringent conditions tagged to it. The repayment burden of loans is also a problem. It becomes very burdensome if it is used for consumption as will be the case of foreign aid sought to meet the consumption needs of the rising population. So also is the case of foreign debt, which is too large for the economy to service. Similar is the consequence of a debt not properly used for productive purpose, so that repayment of the principal and the service charges becomes difficult.

Such debts become deadweight for generations to come. The alternative of foreign direct investment, i.e., equity capital, though the better proposition than loans, cannot be very helpful. This is for the simple reason that this can never be large enough to substitute for domestic saving substantially. All in all, the consequences of a rapidly rising population are certainly unfavourable for capital formation.

In short, it can be said that there is very close relationship between capital formation and growth of population. If there is more capital formation, usually there is a better living standard, higher than the one needed. Population is likely to be a hindrance in the process of capital formation and for population, capital is unavoidably needed.

3. *Impact on Land Resource*

It is obvious that the land of the nation and its underground resources do not increase, therefore, as the population increases the proportion of per capita land decreases and if natural resources are not used properly, then the people face difficulties.

In considering the land area in relation to population, one considers the density of population, i.e., the number of persons per square kilometer. This is very high and has risen rapidly in the past. The population density of India in 2001 was 324 per sq. km. It was 274 in 1991. It has increased rapidly from 216 in 1981. In 1951, it was 117. It means that during the last 50 years, it has almost tripled. As compared to the density of population in the beginning of the century at 77, the present density is more than three times. Not only that, the land-man ratio in general is bad; it is worse when we consider the population in relation to agricultural land. In 1911, the per head availability of land for cultivation was 1.1 acre, which had fallen to almost half of that at 0.6 acre in 1971 and was further down to 0.26 in 1978. This rising pressure of population on agricultural land has led to serious consequences, which are following:

(i) It has obstructed improvements in agriculture. The subdivision and fragmentation of agricultural holdings are the direct results of this pressure on land. It has also sapped the capacity and willingness of cultivators to improve upon agricultural practices.

(ii) In the absence of improvement in agriculture, there has not been any large increase in the amount of farm-work. As a result, we find widespread disguised unemployment and under-employment in the agricultural sectors.

(iii) The consequence is associated with the widening gap between the fast rising demand for various food articles on account of growing population and slower rise in the output of food-articles, partly caused by rise in population. In these circumstances, the country has often been forced to import food on a large-scale, causing serious defect in the balance of payment.

In addition to per capita losses, population growth can lead to degradation of cropland, reducing its productivity or even eliminating it from production.

As a country's population density increases and good farmland becomes scarce, poor farmers are forced to use ecologically vulnerable land, such as hillside and tropical forest. In the Philippines, for example, hillside agriculture land has considerably increased from 1960, and it was 30 per cent in 1987. Because it is highly erodible, hillside land is easily damaged. Worldwide, some 160 million hectares hillside farmland comprising 11 per cent of total cropland were characterised in 1989 as "severely eroded". Similarly, population pressure can force peasants to over-farm the poor soils of tropical forests.

Finally, population pressure on a fixed base of land can result in rural landlessness. In Bangladesh, for example, landlessness among rural households rose from 35 per cent in 1960 to 53 per cent in the early 1990s. Interestingly, Bangladesh is regarded as a success in slowing population expansion, as its growth rate declined from 2.8 per cent in the late 1970s to 1.5 per cent in the early 1990s. But its success came too late to prevent the increase in rural landlessness, highlighting the need to work sooner rather than later for population stabilisation.

It is obvious that in India, high density and rapidly rising population do not contribute to progress, but create difficulties for economic development.

4. *Impact on Natural Capital*

Natural capital of a nation means natural resources of that nation, which get affected adversely with over-growth of population and in proper exploitation of these resources.

Large population does much harm to the capital given to us by Nature. In fact, much degradation of Nature's capacity to support life has already taken place. No doubt, in developed countries the same has happened. But in these countries, it is the wrong kind of development that has impaired the natural capital. It is the reckless exploitation of natural resources that has been responsible for this state of affairs in the developed countries. To an extent, the same thing is happening in India too, as we follow the same technologies in production in several modern sectors of the economy.

However, in India, the large population itself is an important cause in reducing the Nature's resources. In India, as elsewhere in other over-populated countries, the pollution levels have been found to be high. Malthusian economists argue that the world of Nature is finite and has a given productive capacity. As such, it cannot accommodate a population larger than its capacity. Of course, it is difficult to say when the population is larger than the Nature's capacity.

However, it is obvious that at present with little development of the country, the existing large population is more than what is desirable. The proof of this assertion is the acute poverty of a massive number of people in the country. In fact, the poverty of the people has also caused much deterioration to the natural resources. The excessive cultivation of land, which it entails, has done much harm to the agricultural soils causing yields to decline. Again, with the shrinking of good land, the poor people have gone in for steeply sloped, erosion—prone hillsides, and semiarid lands. In such lands, degradation has been more rapid. The crop-yields on cleared fields go down sharply after a few years.

The degraded lands take on such form as desertification, erosion and salinisation or water-logging. Forests, too, have been spoiled by large-scale tree felling by the poor for use as firewood. As a result, the forests, which are the richest ecosystems in terms of biomass and biodiversity on land, have been much eroded. This is upsetting their ecological function of regulating water, supporting plant and animal life, etc. All this is bound to reduce the development potential of the country.

5. *Impact on Food Supply*

Ever since Malthus wrote his 'Essay on Population', attention was focused on the problem of population versus food supply. The relationship between the growth in world population and the grain harvest has shifted over the last half-century, neatly dividing this period into two distinct eras. The global trends conceal widely divergent developments among countries; contrasts that can be seen for the world's two most populous nations—India and China. What happened in China and India is the story of developing countries in general. The overwhelming majority have achieved substantial, if not dramatic, grains in their grain harvests over the last half-century. The slower growth in the world grain harvest since 1984 is due to lack of new land and slower growth in irrigation and fertilizer use. There is no doubt that per capita cultivated area is gradually on the decline in India. Between 1921 and 1991, the cultivated area per capita dropped from 1.11 acres to 0.47 acres, indicating a fall of 58 per cent. To compensate for this fall in cultivated land-man ratio, it is imperative that efforts be made to raise productivity.

Irrigated areas per person, after expanding by 30 per cent from 1950 until 1978, has declined by four per cent since then, as growth in the irrigated area has fallen behind that of the production.

According to the Planning Commission of India, the main reason of our food problem is the growth rate of population, which is greater than the food production. Population of India has increased about one per cent annually, whereas the food production has increased by 0.65 per cent.

According to an estimate of the UN, the population and food production were increasing by 78 and 118 per cent in developing nations up to 1980 due to the present fertility rate and 9.10 per cent annual increase in income. The demand of food will increase by 238 per cent due to increase of three per cent in income. Production of cereals has increased by 54.77 per cent within a period of 15 years, whereas net availability of increased cereals has increased only by 50.35 per cent.

The protein deficiency, which is generally caused by low caloric intake due to non availability of enough food, will keep the major section of population unnourished or undernourished. The food and caloric deficiency retards not only physical growth of child, but mental growth is also affected up to some extent.

Now that the frontiers of agricultural settlement have disappeared, future growth in grain production must come almost entirely from raising land productivity. Unfortunately, this is becoming more difficult. After rising at 2.1 per cent a year from 1950 to 1990, the annual increase in land productivity dropped to barely one per cent from 1990 to 1997. The challenge for the world's farmers is the reverse this decline at a time when crop-land area per person is shrinking, the amount of irrigation water per person is dropping, and the crop yield response to additional fertilizer use is falling.

6. *Impact on Consumers*

India's population can be broadly divided into productive consumers and unproductive consumers. The term productive consumer is being used for that part of the population, which contributes to national income. In other words, it signifies the labour force of the country. Unproductive consumers comprise persons, who are not engaged in employment. Broadly speaking, children, old persons and a part of the population in the age group one to 15 years and above 60 years, who do not seek employment, are included among non-productive consumers.

Table 4.1: Productive and Unproductive Consumers in India

Years	*Total Working Population (Productive Consumers)*		*Total Non-Working Population (Un-productive Consumers)*	
	Million	*Percent*	*Million*	*Percent*
1961	183	43.0	256	57.0
1971	175	34.2	372	65.0
1981	220	37.6	464	62.4

From the above Table 4.1, it is obvious that the ratio of working to non-working population has deteriorated during 1961-81. While in 1961, unproductive consumers totaled about 256 million, in 1981, their number stood at about 464 million. Not only in absolute terms, even the proportion of non-productive consumers in the total population has gone up from 57 per cent in 1961 to 62 per cent in 1981. However, the ratio of working population during 1981-91 has remained unchanged, though the total number of non-workers has risen to 529 million. Forty-two per cent of the total population being in the age-group 0-14, the child component of unproductive consumers is roughly 80 per cent of the non-working population. A high and increasing population of children increases the burden of the care of the young through nutrition, medical care, public health and education.

Economists calculate the dependency load of population of a country with reference to the contribution to production of consumption needs. Ideally, it should be like this: adult in the productive age-group, i.e., 15-59 as one; children in the age-group 0-14 as one-third; and aged person (60 and above) as one-half (in the case of India in 1981, the population was composed of 40% children, 54% adults and 6% aged persons). Then, for every 100 adults of productive age, there is a ratio of 131 consumer equivalents. In a developed country, where the age composition is in favour of the productive age-group (on an average, 23% children, 67 % adults and 10% aged), the equivalent of 100 adults in the productive age-group is 119 consumer units. It is obvious that the age composition of population in a country like India indicates 10 per cent more dependency load as compared to an advanced country like the USA.

7. *Impact on Employment*

An overpopulated country has to face the serious problem of unemployment and under-employment. Since mid-century, the world's labour force has more than doubled from 1.2 billion to 2.7 billion people, outstripping the growth in job creation. As a result, the United Nations International Labour Organisation estimates that nearly one billion people, approximately 30 per cent of the global work force, are unemployed or under employed (working but not earning enough to meet basic needs). Over the next half-century, the world will need to create more than 1.9 billion jobs, all of them in the developing world, just to maintain the current levels of employment.

As economists often note, while population growth may boost labour demand (through economic activity and demand for goods), it will most definitely boost labour supply. During the next 50 years, almost 40 million people will enter the global labour force—defined as those between the age group of 15 and 65 seeking work each year. As the children of today represent the workers of tomorrow, the interaction between population growth and jobs is the most acute in nations with young populations. Nations, such as Peru, Mexico, Indonesia, and Zambia with more than half of their population being below the age of 25, will feel the burden of this labour flood. Nowhere is the employment challenge greater than in Africa, where at least 40 per cent of the population lives in absolute poverty. Although eight million people entered the sub-Saharan work force in 1997, by 2030, this resource-scarce region will have to absorb more than 17 million new entrants each year. Over the next half-century, Nigeria's labour force is projected to grow by 246 per cent and Ethiopia's will soar by 337 per cent – both faster than the growth of the general population. At current growth rates, the size of the labour force in sub-Saharan Africa will be more than triple by 2050.

As a result of unprecedented population growth and increasing acceptance of female participation in the work force, the number of people seeking jobs in the Middle East and North Africa, a region already plagued by double-digit unemployment rates, will double in the next 50 years. In Algeria, where employment stands at 200 per cent, the labour force is growing at a staggering 4.2 per cent annually, and the number seeking work will more than double by 2050. Egypt alone will need to create 26 million more jobs by 2050 as its total population hits 115 million. Nations throughout Asia will also see phenomenal increases in the numbers seeking work, including Pakistan, where the work force will grow from 70 million in 1998 to 205 million by 2050.

Over the next 25 years, India will add nearly 10 million people to its work force each year. During the same period, China will add nearly six million annually due to population growth alone, compounding the work shortages caused by the current flood of migrants from China's coastal cities and by massive layoffs—as estimated, more than 30 million state-run operations are scaled back. Nations are hard-pressed to educate and train rapidly growing numbers of young people in marketable skills for the global workplace. Moreover, meeting the basic needs of the growing population draws back scarce foreign exchange and other resources from investments in education and job creation.

Surplus farmland once served as a traditional source of employment for growing populations, as new land could be ploughed to generate work and income. However, global per capita grain land has dropped by half-and considerably more in certain nations-since 1950.

There are different types of unemployment in India and other developing countries due to increasing population. Following are the main types of unemployment.

(i) *Structural Unemployment*: Basically, India's unemployment is structural in nature. It is associated with the inadequacy of productive capacity to create enough jobs for all those able and willing to work. In India, not only is productive capacity (largely capital stock) much below the needed quantity, it is also found increasing at a slow rate. As against this, additions to labour-force are being made at a fast rate on account of the rapidly growing population. Thus, while new productive jobs are on the increase, the rate of increase being low, the absolute number of unemployed persons is rising from year to year.

(ii) *Disguised Employment*: Disguised unemployment means unemployment that is not open for everyone to see; it remains invisible. In Indian villages, where most of the unemployment exists in this form, people are found to be apparently engaged in agricultural activities. But such employment is mostly a work-sharing device, i.e., the existing work is shared, howsoever large may be the number of workers. In such situation, even if many workers are withdrawn, the same work will continue to be done by fewer people. It follows that all workers are not needed to maintain the existing level of production. The contribution of such labourers to production is thus zero to zero or near zero.

(iii) In the case of disguised unemployment, everyone only seems to be fully employed. It is so because a larger number of workers than actually required are sharing a given amount of work. As such, it appears that nobody is without work. But this, of course, conceals the fact that there is no full employment, as the workers are not working to their full capacity. The proof of this is that the output does not fall if a part of the labour-force is withdrawn. In the case of full employment, however, all the workers contribute to output and a withdrawal of a part of the labour-force will cause a fall in production.

(iv) *Under-Employment*: It is a situation under which employed people are contributing to production less than they are capable of. For example, a diploma holder in engineering, if for want of an appropriate job, starts shoe shining, he may be said to be under-employed. Apparently, he may be deemed as working and earning in a productive activity and in this sense contributing something to production. But in reality, he is not working according to his capability, nor to his full capacity. He is, therefore, not fully employed. Here too, his under-employment is disguised.

(v) *Open Unemployment*: Under this category fall those, who have no work to do. They are able to work and are also willing to work. But there is no work for them. Such an underemployment is in the nature of involuntary idleness. They are to be found partly in rural areas, but very largely in urban areas.

Thus, the increasing population creates the burning problem of unemployment. No country can solve the problem of unemployment without reducing the population growth.

8. *Impact on Poverty*

Employment is the key to obtain food, housing, health services and education in addition to providing self-respect and self-fulfillment.

People do not get employment due to increasing population. Another thing is that food production is not increasing with the rate of population growth. Therefore, food is not sufficient for the increasing population. Thus, growth of population influences poverty. According to a survey, which was held in 1999-2000, 28.6 per cent people are below the poverty line. And according to the World Bank report, 35.3 per cent people of India are under the international poverty line. It means 35.3 per cent people do not get sufficient food, which is the basic need of human being. Poverty is a hindrance in economic development. Poverty is an economic problem as well as social too.

9. *Impact on Technical Advancement*

Population growth also influences technical advancement and, in fact, the whole process of gaining and imparting technical know-how. If the growing population is ambitious and literate, then there will be an attempt to have new technical know-how and vice-versa. If, in a country, the population is growing, then it is better if labour oriented techniques are adopted in that country; on the other hand, if such a country adopts capital oriented techniques, then the production will not only be costly, but such a nation shall not be in a position to solve unemployment problem for its growing population. It is, therefore, desirable that the developing countries should adopt labour oriented techniques and developed countries capital oriented, though no country can abandon any technique altogether. If however, a less developed country has less population, then it may be possible for that country to adopt capital oriented techniques as well and that might prove useful as well. Technical advancement can even be rapid and the problem of unemployment in that country may not pose a very serious threat. Such country can do its economic development easily.

Thus, there are adverse impact of population growth on economic development. The size and the rate of population growth has an important bearing on the economic development of a country. If the population is too small, it does not afford full scope for specialisation or division of labour, nor a sufficient market for the goods produced in the country. If on the other hand, population is too large, then also it is a great impediment to economic growth. It is a serious hindrance to capital formation. The feeding of a huge population leaves little scope for saving, and saving is very essential for economic growth, because capital formation is the very crux of the process of economic growth.

Ashok Mehta has very aptly remarked that population growth is like a thief, who robs us of the benefit of economic development. Hence, increase in population swallows up the major part of increase in national income on account of which, there can be no significant rise in the per capita income and in the level of livings. This is what has happened in India in the era of planned economic development.

Thus, it is clear that increasing population is a great obstacle in the economic development of developing countries like India. Hence, population should be of a proper or optimum size.

Impact of Population Growth on Social Development

In the previous section, we discussed the impact of population growth on economic development and its serious consequences for economic development. There is also adverse impact of population growth on social development. Any country cannot develop socially due to increasing population. Many empirical studies observed that over-populated countries have more social problems. Government of these countries failed to provide basic needs of the people. Poverty, illiteracy, unemployment, problem of housing, high infant mortality rates are the indications of social backwardness of over-populated countries. Following are the adverse impact of increasing population on social development.

1. *Poverty*

Poverty can be defined as a social phenomenon where a section of the society is unable to fulfill even its basic necessities of life. When a substantial segment of a society is deprived of the minimum level of living and continues to exist at bare subsistence level, then the society is said to be plagued with mass poverty. The countries of the third world exhibit invariably the existence of mass poverty. Rapidly increasing population is the main cause of poverty.

Attempts have been made in all societies to define poverty, but all of them are conditioned by the vision of minimum or good life obtaining in different forms than those in India because the average person is able to afford a much higher level of living in United States. Poverty can be measured in terms of the 'absolute' standard of poverty expressed in the country. The deprivation of a significant section of the society of minimum basic needs in the face of a luxurious life for the elite classes makes poverty more glaring.

Dr. V.M. Dandekar and Mr. Nilkantha Rath estimated the value of the diet with 2,250 calories as the desired minimum level of nutrition. They suggest that whereas the Planning Commission accepts ₹ 20 (according to 1960-61 prices) per capita per month (or ₹ 240 per annum) as the minimum desirable standard, it would not be fair to use this figure for both the urban and the rural areas. Dandekar and Rath, therefore, suggested somewhat lower minimum for rural population, i.e., ₹ 180 per capita per annum and somewhat higher minimum, ₹ 270 per capita per annum for the urban population at 1960-61 prices.

The World Bank, in its country study titled, "India: Poverty, Employment and Social Services (1989)" has also made use of the same procedure as adopted by the Planning Commission. The poverty line is the expenditure level at which minimum calorie intake and indispensable nonfood purchases are assumed. Poverty lines of ₹ 49.1 and 56.6 per capita per month were defined by the Planning Commission for rural and urban areas for the period 1973-74. The World Bank used an alternative method of estimating poverty proportion applying a deflator series developed by the NSS and the Indian Statistical Institute to calculate updated poverty lines (in current prices) of ₹ 55.2 (rural) for 1983.

In Amartya Sen's view, poverty is not just a matter of being relatively poorer than others, but of not having some basic opportunities of material well being that he termed as the failure to have certain minimum "capabilities". The capabilities are of different kinds, i.e., being free from starvation, from hunger, from under-nourishment, from participating in community life, etc. According to Dr. Sen, poverty is not a matter of only income, but it also refers to the failure to achieve certain minimum capabilities. He emphasised that a person must have basic capabilities to obtain the elementary physical necessities, such as nourishment, clothing, shelter, etc. Because of capability failure, a poor person is deprived of amenities and facilities, such as health, services, education, etc. Even though there may be sufficient income, a poor person may be deprived of these basic needs and services. So, social and educational conditions become important to determine the degree of poverty in a society.

The World Bank has given social indicators of poverty in the book entitled, '2005' World Development Indicators.' According to World Bank, prevalence of child malnutrition, under-five mortality rate, child immunisation rate, contraceptive use prevalence, births attended by skilled health staff are the social indicators of poverty.

After knowing the serious problem of poverty, the developing world has been engaged in the task of eliminating poverty for last several decades or so. Since the World Summit for Social Development (1995) was held in Copenhagen, targets were fixed for reduction of poverty and the participants made commitments to reduce poverty within a time-bound framework. The United Nation's Secretary General, in his report entitled, "Implementation of reviewed the progress made by the developing countries in various regions in the eradication's of poverty.

2. *Quality of Life*

In 2001, India's population was 102.70 crores, which is increasing almost by two per cent each year. This population is much more than the geographical size of the nation in relation to other nations of the world. It is a matter of grave concern. Hence, it is essential to understand the impact of population growth on the quality of human life.

Quality of life can be defined as "optimal satisfaction of human needs, the organic needs, the special needs and the individual needs for self-realisation."

Survival is the most basic of instincts in all animals including mammals of which homosephians is sub-species. Food, clothing, shelter and basic health care are the major variable closely related to the survival in any human being. Once survival is attained through various protective and innovative measures, man bettered himself and the reality of survival was subsequently improved.

Quality of life means when survival is the most pressing problem before us. The rapidly rising population of our country without concomitant socio-economic development is a serious threat to our survival. In the battle for survival, quality remains the privilege of a fortunate few. How could a country survive with a fast growing population that would, no doubt, outstrip any economic and social development.

High infant-mortality rate, squalor of slums, under-nourishment, respiratory diseases, etc. are observed to be general indicators of the lot of fairly large sections of the population of our country. The quality of life is meaningful to those, who know about it. For example, economic resources and development programmes have been utilised to feed, educate and maintain good health, but the rising number of births with limited resources dilute the quality of these programmes, which, in turn, affect the quality of our life. This has been the underlying reason for the failure of all development programmes, not only in India, but in many developing countries.

The quality of life is partially determined by the biosphere or the ecological niche, i.e., ocean fisheries, forests, grassland and cropland, without which life with quality cannot possibly be imagined. With our triumphant technological and scientific achievements, we are disrupting the ecological niche. We are not simply exploiting species for our own use, but we are making many thousands species extinct. We are destroying our coastal fishery nurseries for our survival needs. It is very important to repair the damaged eco-system throughout the world for the survival of mankind with improved quality of life.

Many developing countries of the world are caught up in the vicious circle of poverty, and whatever economic development programmes are introduced for bettering the quality of life, their impact is immediately eliminated by the demands of the rapidly growing population.

In terms of quality of life, already an extremely serious situation exists in respect to the existence of mankind. His very existence on this earth is being threatened. Men should accept the challenge of promoting self-reliance amongst all sections of the society and march towards the universal humanist search for real meaning of life. We have still to go a long way in achieving the optimal satisfaction of our survival needs and what is called quality of life.

3. *Urbanisation*

The rising trend towards urbanisation are reflected in larger rise in urban population, and concentration of the major proportion of urban population in larger cities. Population growth is the important factor of urbanisation. The birth-rate is higher than the death-rate in the urban areas. This is probably higher than rural, and because of the health and medical facilities, the net survival rate is also higher. The birth-rate in the urban areas in 1971 has been estimated at 30.1 (per thousand) with death-rate being at 9.7 (per thousand). In 1978, the birth rate declined to 27.8. The death-rate fell slightly to 9.4. This has caused the population growth rate to be high because of large difference between the birth and death rates. The low level of death-rate is due largely to such reasons as greater medical and health services, good water supply and sanitation that reduce the incidence of water borne diseases, etc. This natural factor must have added a lot to the phenomenal population growth in the urban areas at 46 per cent during the 1971-81 decade as against 19 per cent rise in rural population, and over 24 per cent in the total population.

Because of increasing population, many people in rural areas have turned to the agricultural sector. Therefore, there is disguised unemployment in the rural area. Lack of employment, lack of opportunities for good education and living in the rural areas have attracted rural people to the urban areas. Hence, rural people migrate to cities and live in slums due to high prices of plots and rented houses. Many social problems are created by urbanisation.

The world's cities are growing faster than its population. Indeed, aside from the growth of population itself, urbanisation is the dominant demographic trend of the century. In 1950, 750 million of the world's people lived in cities. By 1996, this has at least tripled to more than 2.6 billion. The number projected to live in cities by 2050 is some 6.5 billion people, which exceeds the current world population. In, 1800 only one city—London had a million people. Today, 326 cities have at least that many people, and there are 14 megacities, those with 10 million each. Rounding off the list in descending order are Mumbai (15 million), Shanghai (14m) Los Angeles (12m). Beijing (11m), Osaka (11m), Lagos (10m), Rio de Janeiro (10m), and New Delhi (10). Measured in terms of annual growth, some cities, such as Lagos, Nigeria, are growing at five per cent a year, while Mumbai is growing at nearly four per cent. The world's urban population as a whole is growing by just over one million people each week.

During the early stages of industrialisation, urbanisation was largely in response to the pull of employment opportunities in cities. More recently, however, the movement from countryside to city has been more the result of rural push than of urban pull. It is a reflection of the lack of opportunity in the countryside, as small plots of lands are divided and then divided again with each passing generation until they become so small that people can no longer make a living from them.

As societies urbanise, the use of basic resources, such as energy and infrastructure rises. The ecology of cities is a continuing challenge to city managers simply because cities require the concentration of huge quantities of water, food, energy, and raw materials. The waste product must then be dispersed or the city will become uninhabitable. As cities become larger, the disposal of residential and industrial wastes becomes ever more challenging.

Partly as a result of the mounting pressure for people to migrate to cities, the growth in urban populations is far out stripping the availability of basic services, such as water, sewerage, transportation, and electricity. As a result, life in urban shanty towns is plagued by poverty, pollution, congestion, homelessness, and unemployment.

4. *Housing*

In the field of housing and city planning, the impact of population growth manifests itself most bluntly. In India, the urban housing shortage is the most tragic. The rural housing deficit in India leads to high demands. The government has not achieved target in providing adequate housing facilities to growing masses so far.

Over the half-century, the world's housing stock has grown roughly in step with population. Yet, for more and more people would wide, adequate and affordable housing remains beyond reach, driving some into substandard dwellings and slums and others onto the street. This situation stands to worsen, for the need for housing worldwide is projected to nearly double over the next 50 years. Although industrial nations currently occupy a disproportionately large share of the world's households relative to their population, virtually all future growth will occur in developing countries, where housing requirement will be more than double by the middle of the twenty-first century. This phenomenal growth would result from the potent synergy between population growth and a shift toward fewer people per household, a trend that is especially pronounced where economic growth is rapid.

HABITAT, the United Nation's Centre for Human Settlements, has projected housing requirements based on roughly 30 per cent reduction in people per household over the next years. These figures are purely statistical estimates and do not consider possible checks in housing growth, such as materials or financial constraints, intensified land competition, or increased poverty. Our own projections assume that household size will indeed decrease, as fertility rates drop and as extended families become more rare, but by a more modest 15 per cent. Over the next 50 years, housing needs in Africa and the Middle East are expected to rise in comparison to Asia, the doubling of households in the region will require nearly 700 million additional homes by 2050.

HABITAT estimates that at least 600 million urban dwellers and more than one billion rural dwellers in Africa, Asia and Latin America live in housing that is "so overcrowded and of such poor quality with such inadequate provision for water, sanitation, drainage, and garbage collection that their lives and their health are continually at risk."

Housing can provide a connection to a supply of fresh water and sanitation facilities. But, as its quality deteriorates, so do these basic amenities. Half of the world's population lives without access to sanitation and nearly this many—2.7 billion—are without a reliable source of safe drinking water. Shortages of housing that provide these basic services are most acute in cities, where rapid urbanisation and high population densities place heightened demands on infrastructure.

The ultimate manifestation of population growth outstripping the supply of housing is homelessness. The United Nations estimates that at least 100 million of the world's people—roughly the same as the population of Mexico—have no home; the number tops one billion if those with insecure or temporary accommodations, such as squatters, are included. In many developing countries, squatter communities are homes to 30-60 per cent of the urban population. There are some 2,50,000 pavement dwellers in Mumbai alone. In Latin America, 'los ninos de la calle' (children of the streets), people, who are born, live and die in the streets—are common in all major cities." Unless the world moves to a lower population trajectory, the ranks of homeless are likely to swell dramatically.

5. *High Infant Mortality Rate*

Increasing population has an impact on infant mortality rate. Developing countries have high infant mortality rates. The problem of unemployment is becoming serious in these countries. Many people live below the poverty line. The high infant mortality rate is more acute among the poor people because of deficient diet, lack of medical facilities, unhealthy living conditions, etc. In many poor families, where the number of children, particularly of the same sex, may be quite high and an additional child may not be much cared for. The mother can be ignorant and may not realise the need of post natal medical care after the birth of child. Parent cannot take care of the children due to poverty. Children are not nourished well. Therefore, high infant mortality is found in populous countries. India has high infant mortality rate. Many demographers observed that high infant mortality rate is the phenomenon of over-populated countries. The infant mortality rate is 7.4 per cent in India, which means that 74 infants out of 1000 die in India.

6. *Education*

In contrast to the food supply challenge posed by the coming wave of population growth, the global need for teachers and classrooms will rise very slowly in the next half-century. In many countries, the school-age population is increasing. They much less rapidly differ for different age strata of the population. It also shows that declining birth rate can take decades to move through an entire population.

Many countries have increasing population of children. Where the countries have not acted to stabilise population, the base of the national population pyramid continues to expand, and the pressure on the educational system will be severe. In the world's ten fastest growing countries, for example, most of which are in Africa and the Middle East; the child-age population will increase, at an average, 93 per cent over the next half century. Africa as a whole will see its school-age population grow by 75 per cent through 2040.

The rapid growth in African population is especially worrisome because of the extra burden it imposes on a region already lagging in education. Only 56 per cent of Africans south of the Sahara are literate, compared with 71 per cent for all developing countries. Few African countries have universal primary education, and secondary education reaches only four to five per cent of African children. Today, educating children is challenging enough; the addition of another three students for every four already there will require heroic investment in education. Today's average student-teacher ratio of 42 in Sub-Sahara Africa will reach 75 by 2040.

Many countries will be challenged to increase funding for education, while ensuring that other worthy sectors also receive the support they need. With 900 million illiterate adults in the world, the case for a renewed commitment to education is easy to make. But competing for these funds are the 840 million chronically hungry and the 1.2 billion without access to a decent toilet.

If national education systems begin to stress life-long learning for a rapidly changing word, as recommended by a 1998 UNESCO report on education in the twenty-first century, then extensive provision for adult education will be necessary, affecting even those countries with shrinking child-age population. Such a development means that countries that started population stabilisation programmes at the earliest will be in the best position to educate their entire citizenry.

India is one of the most populous countries. Hence, we have very large school going population for which we do not have enough infrastructure, i.e., school buildings, teachers, etc., and because of this, we have not been able to provide compulsory basic education, though there are other aspects too.

When there is a large proportion of children and young people, the Governments find it difficult to muster resources for educating the children, much less for providing the quality of education necessary for enabling each citizen to be productive or enlightened.

With approximately 50 per cent of India's population below 18 years of age, even tremendous expansion of education has proved to be quite inadequate. This is the statistical picture; perhaps the reality is gloomier. One shudders to think of the state of affairs in the next two or three decades when the social demand for education will be much greater. Again, population growth has proved to be a major obstacle in the attainment of qualitative improvement in education. Qualitative improvement requires facilities for innovation, conditions conducive to experimentation, well-equipped laboratories and a cadre of researchers.

However, because of population pressure, the bulk of the available resources in most countries of this region go into the opening of new schools and, consequently, there is hardly any scope for educational innovations and improvements.

Some studies carried out recently to explore the impact of population growth and change upon educational development have indicated that major reduction in birth rates is vital to both quantitative and qualitative progress of education in developing countries.

It is clear that the impact of population growth on education is very adverse. Hence, it is the need of time to keep strict control on the population growth.

7. *Natural Recreation Areas*

Population growth during the last 50 years has made it difficult to set aside and conserve natural areas. Another half-century of population growth will put even more pressure on protected areas, as formerly small and distant settlements encroach on these sites and the number of people (both local and visitors), who use these explodes.

National parks, forests, wildlife reserves, beaches, and other protected areas offer sanctuary to various habitats and indigenous communities, in addition to providing resources for local people. In an urbanising world, these sites provide an opportunity for healthy interaction with the natural environment, as well as rare serenity. Tremendous growth in the population puts pressure on the National Park region, a reserve that was beyond the city's periphery only a decade ago. With projected growth of 60 per cent in the population in the next 20 years, Mumbai may soon swallow up more distant areas. On every continent, human encroachment has reduced both the size and the quality of natural recreation areas.

In nations where rapid population growth has outstripped the carrying capacity of local resources, the protected areas have become especially vulnerable. Although in industrial nation these areas are synonymous with camping, hiking, and picnics in the country, in Asia, Africa and Latin America, most National Parks, forests, and reserves are inhabited or used for natural resources by the local population.

An assessment by the World Conservation Union—IUCN of 30 protected sites in the developing world shows that these areas now act as magnets, attracting people to the rich oasis of water, fuel, food and other resources they contain. Population growth rates in and around these areas is typically two percentage points above the national average—largely as a result of immigration from resource starved areas.

Coastal recreation areas, including beaches, may be the most burdened by the formidable combination of population growth and migration. All but one of the world's 15 largest cities—Mexico City—are coastal, and all of these cities will grow in the decades ahead. Whether it takes the form of expanding shanty towns in Kingston, Jamaica, or sprawling tract housing in Southern California, virtually all the growth and movement in population in the next 50 years will occur in densely populated coastal corridors.

In Nations are already struggling to meet basic human needs, the prospect of establishing additional protected areas becomes increasingly slim. Throughout India, for example, while the national Government designates areas as protected, States and local Government work to de-reserve these sites so that the resources can be harnessed to meet the needs of additional 18 million Indians each year.

As discussed above, all the adverse impacts of population become hurdles in economic and social development. Hence, it is the need of the age to control population growth. For this, Dr. Babasaheb Ambedkar suggested the measures for birth control about 67 years ago.

NOTES

1. Raimomndo Cagiano de Azevedo (1987), (Editor) *Population, Aid and Development*, International Union for the Scientific Study of Population, p. 23.
2. Sharma, Yogendra (2005), *Population Education*, Kanishka Publishers and Distributors, Delhi, p. 171.
3. Hirschan, Albert O. (1958), *The Strategy of Economic Development*, Yale, New Heaven, p. 18.
4. Lewis, Arthur W. (1954), *Economic Development and Unlimited Supply of Labour*, The Manchester School, May 1954. Reprinted in Agarwal, A.N. and Singh, S.P. (1958), *The Economics of Under-development*, p. 400.

5

Dr. Ambedkar's Views and Their Relevance in Modern Age

The most important problem India is facing today is the size and growth of its population. The Census 2001 has shown that the population of India is estimated at 102 crores, 87 lakh, 37 thousand, 436 as on 1 March 2001. India accounts for a meager 2.4 per cent of the world's surface area of 135.79 million sq. km. Yet, it supports and sustains a whopping 16.7 per cent of the world population. In the 50 years since 1951, the population of the country has increased from 36.11 crores to 102.87 crores. The average annual exponential growth rate between 1991 and 2001 is recorded at 1.93 per cent, which means that the present growth rate may be somewhat lesser. The net addition to our total population during the last decade was about 181 million. As the fertility rate is falling, it may be safe to assume that on an average, we may be adding about 17 million people every year to our population during the 1991-2001 decade.

On this basis, the population of India is likely to reach about 119.70 crores by 2011. Beyond this period, the population projections vary depending upon the assumptions made about fertility and mortality rates. However, generally it is felt that India's population will reach about 140 crores by the year 2026.[1] Population projection beyond a period of 25 years becomes more unreliable due to a number of reasons.

Thus, in the twenty five years after 2001, we are going to add about 37.3 crores more people in our population, which is about 133 per cent of current population of the USA and 176 per cent of the present population of Indonesia, the countries coming next to China and India in population size now. A comparison with China's population is more relevant in the case of India. China's population was estimated at 127 crores, 80 lakhs in 2000. It is now growing at about 0.95 per cent annually, i.e., an addition of about 12 million people every year compared to the addition of 17 million people in the case of India.[2] Thus, India is now adding every year about five million more people than China. At this rate, there is a possibility that India may overtake China in population size by the middle of the current century.

Indian population is still growing very fast; the pressure of numbers on the natural resources of the country is bound to grow. The density of population has increased from 117 persons per sq. km. in 1951 to 324 persons in 2001. High population density States like Bihar (880) and Uttar Pradesh (689) are now witnessing rapid growth in population, which may worsen the already very poor social and demographic indicators in these States. The population pressure will badly affect the per capita availability of curable land, water for drinking and housing. In the area of health care facilities, we are still operating on the basis of the 1991 population. But even on that basis, there are large infrastructural and human resource gaps prevailing mostly in the high population growth regions of the country.

India has the largest concentration of the poor, the illiterate, the sick and the unemployed in the world. We have made some progress in terms of literacy rate, especially at the female literacy front in the last decade; still about 30 crore people in India can neither read nor write. In short, no unbiased observer can deny the fact that uncontrolled growth of India's population during the last five decades has acted as a drag on the country's effort to develop and improve the quality of life of its people. The population explosion will continue to remain the single major hindrance in the path of the country's progress for many more decades to come.

It is a reality of India regarding population growth. Dr. Babasaheb Ambedkar was aware about the population explosion that is why he had warned against the alarming population growth. Unfortunately, his views went unheard and unheeded. Members of the Bombay Assembly opposed his views related to birth control and resolution regarding measures for birth control.

Recently, the Rashtriya Swayamsevak Sangha (RSS) Sarsanghchalak, K.S. Sudarshan has opposed the efforts to reduce population growth. Mr. Sudarshan called upon his fellow Hindus to go forth and multiply with the slogan, "Produce at least three children each. Not less than three, you should produce as many as possible (*teen se kam nahi, app jyada kar sakein utna achchha*)." Religious Demography of India brought out by the Centre for Policy Studies on 18 November 2005 in Delhi.[3]

He asked Hindus not to get into the trap of slogans like, "*Hum do, humare do*" and "*hum do, humara ek*" so as to keep the demographic composition of India intact.

To underline this point, Sudarshan said that a couple with 12 sons was likely to be survived by a 1,200 strong progeny after 120 years. The one with 11 sons would have 1,100 successors. While couples with 2 sons would show a zero increase. "The family line of people with one son would be snapped," he added.

It is clear that Hindu leaders like Sudarshan oppose birth control even today. Mahatma Gandhi shared same type of views during his life time. There is no change in the thought of religious leaders of Hinduism. Today, everybody knows the danger of population explosion, but these religious leaders are asking their followers to increase their population. We can understand very well how Dr. Ambedkar showed his courage and raised the problem of population growth.

India and China have been facing the problem of increasing population. India's religious leaders advise people to produce more and more children. But at the same time, China's Councilor and Secretary General of the State Council, Hua Jianmin said that, "The one-child norm should be kept on so that the country can push forward family planning reforms."[4]

"In the early 1970s, a Chinese couple had an average of 5.8 children. The number has since dropped to 1.8, placing China in the world's low birth rate club. But given China's large population base of 1.3 million, keeping the birth rate at a low level remains a very important mission in the country," Hua Jianmin said.

He shared these thoughts in a letter addressed to the Conference on the Framing of New Mechanisms for National Population and Family Planning held from September 16 to 18, 2005. He said that it was imperative that China kept to its current family planning policy during the key Eleventh Five Year Plan time starting from 2006.

Hua Jianmin urged the Governments and Family Planning Commissions to deal with the population issue by focusing on an all round development of humans, sticking to the practice that the Government leader should take responsibility of family planning and keeping the planning network unchanged.

He said that China should step up its efforts to improve the family planning work mechanism, which emphasises management according to law, self-governance of villages or urban residents, quality services, policy impetus and comprehensive management during the Tenth Five Year Plan period from 2001 to 2005. The conference suggested new mechanism after studying the experience during the Tenth Five-year Plan period. It has decided that most regions of the country should set up such a mechanism by the year 2010 to handle the population issue in a comprehensive way.

Though some religious leaders, like Mr. Sudarshan opposed birth control, many political leaders, social scientists and social reformers have realised the importance of birth control. Therefore, except some religious leaders, all the people are the supporters of birth control.

Population Policy in India—The Background

In 1916, Pyare Kishen Wattal published his book entitled *The Population Problem in India* advocating limitation of family size. Prof. R.D. Karve opened the birth control clinic in Poona in 1923. In 1928, with the support of many influential persons, including high court judges, a neo-Malthusian League was formed in Madras city. It published a journal in 1929 emphasising the need to control the birth rate. In 1930, the native State of Mysore, with its enlightened 'Prime Minister', opened the first Government clinic in Bangalore, although it attracted few clients. In 1932, the All India Women's Conference, during its Lucknow session, passed a resolution recommending that men and women should be instructed in methods of birth control in recognised clinics.[5] In 1935, the society for the study and promotion of family hygiene was formed with Smt. Cowasji Jehangir as its first president. In 1936, Dr. A.P. Pillai started his training courses in family planning.

Dr. Babasaheb Ambedkar referred to the problem of over-population in the election manifesto of his Independent Labour Party in 1936 and said that over-population was the major cause of poverty in India. It was the first political party in India, which incorporated this view in its election manifesto. It was a historical event when Dr. Babasaheb Ambedkar moved non-official resolution regarding measures for birth control on behalf of the Independent Labour Party in Bombay Assembly in 1938.

In 1938, Subhash Chandra Bose, President of the Indian National Congress, advocated a restriction on India's population size. He set up the National Planning Committee (NPC) under the Chairmanship of Pandit Jawaharlal Nehru, who became the first Prime Minister of Independent India, to prepare a plan for the social and economic development of India after it gained independence. In 1939, the 'Birth Control World-Wide' in Uttar Pardesh and Matru Sewa Sangh, Ujjain, in Madhya Pradesh opened birth control clinics. In 1940, Mr. P.N. Sapru successfully moved a resolution in the Council of Sates for establishment of birth control clinics.

About this time, Smt. Rena Dutta toured extensively to organise birth control campaigns on behalf of the Family Planning Association, London.

The report of the sub-committee, reviewed by the parent body in May, 1940 led the NPC to resolve that "measures for the improvement of quality of population and limiting excessive population pressure" were 'necessary' and that in the interest of social, economic, family happiness and national planning, family planning and of children, such measures are essential and the State should adopt a policy to encourage them." While considering it desirable "to lay stress on self-control, as well as knowledge of cheap and safe methods of birth control", the Committee supported the establishment of birth control clinics and made efforts to "prevent the use or advertisement of harmful methods". The latter caveat presumably referred to abortion.[6]

The NPC supported the "gradual raising of the marriage age", "discouragement of polygamy", and an eugenic programme including the sterilisation of persons sufferings from transmissible diseases, such as insanity or epilepsy", but it did not specifically endorse the sub-committee's suggestion of promoting the idea of spacing births two to four years apart and limiting the total number of children in a family to four.

These events are noted here at length because they were reflected in the development in post-independence India. For many years, the leaders admired the then apparent Soviet success in planned economic development and wanted to develop a similar socialist society.[7] By emulating certain aspects of the Soviet system, they believed that India's poverty could be quickly eradicated. India's leftist political leaders often cited Marxist writings on population and the pro-nationalist policies of the USSR to illustrate the need to stress development over population control as the urgent national imperative.

The Health Survey and Development Committee was appointed in 1943 by the Government of India under the Chairmanship of Sir Joseph Bhore. The Committee recommended the provision of birth control service, but mainly for health reasons. The Committee considered the deliberate limitation of family size to be "advisable" and noted that it could not be achieved through self-control to any material extent. The Committee was divided over the issue of a state supported programme to promote birth control, but it supported state control over: 1) The manufacture and sale of contraceptive; 2) Public assistance in research for developing a safe and effective contraceptive; and 3) Continuous study of population problem and its related factors.

This is the background of the population policy in India. Population was increasing day by day. Hence, population problem became serious. The Government recognised the importance of birth control.

Population Policy and Family Planning in India

Before discussing about population policy in India, it is necessary to define, what is population policy? According to Gunnar Myrdal, "A population policy can be nothing less than a social policy at large".[8] In his opinion, a population programme must work itself into the whole fabric of social life. In the population policy are covered programmes and polices relating to increase and decrease of death and birth rates, increase in population growth rate and distribution of population, etc.

J.J. Spengler said, "Under national population policy are covered all such population problems, which influence either quality or distribution of population. Population policy can be both explicit as well as implicit. Under explicit policy, we solved population problems, whereas in implicit policy, population problems are solved under some economic, social or political policy." Mr. Spengler has also said that population policy can be formulated with immediate as well as long term objectives. The objects of such policy can also be quantitative, qualitative as well as spatial.

According to Frank W. Note Stein, the main objective of national population policy today is to ensure that there is reasonable gap between the fall of death and birth rates.

Paul Meadows has said that the national population policy should have norms as well as methodology. According to him, the norms should be that birth of the children should be well planned and whether a child should or should not be born that should be planned and kept optional. He also said that it should be possible to given, then, proper education and maintain good health for them. The norms should help in keeping population at a reasonable level. In methodology, he suggested that there should be improvement in production, increased availability of food supplies, sufficient storage of food, late marriage, tax on producing more children, etc.

According to R.R. Mukherjee, "A democratic population policy will accept the increased supply, but it will neglect the possibility of reducing demands. Anti democratic population policies have opportunistically followed lines of action suggested in both groups." But D.V. Glass has rather very appropriately said that it was wrong to believe that there could be a national population policy. In fact, there could not be a universal national policy and even a nation could not pursue a national policy for all times to come. It will have to change with changing times.

Thus, population policy is a very comprehensive term, which includes all efforts, which are made by any Government to control and change the population structure. UNESCO Population Commission report and Ad hoc Consultative Group of Experts on population policy, 23 March 1972 includes measures and programmes, which contribute to the achievements of economic, social, demographic, political and other collective's goals through critical demographic variables, e.g., size and growth of population and its geographical distribution. If population policy is taken in its broadest sense, it will include birth, death and growth rates; internal and international migrations; and social, ethical, economic and biological factors, which affect the population.

After getting independence, Indian planners realised that the rapid growth of population and the absolute population size would reduce through the economic development of the country. India was, therefore, one of the first countries, which launched a plan of economic development, side by side population control by bringing about a change in family size and fertility reduction.

The growing feeling that population growth was at the very roots of our poverty was foremost in the mind of the then Prime Minister, Pandit Jawaharlal Nehru. Myrdal, while recognising this fact, pays him a tribute in the following words.[9]

> "Nehru was at some time or other hospitable to most of these ideas. It is true that he spoke out clearly against Gandhi's insistence on continence as the only acceptable means of birth control, and that he never retreated on this score. He occasionally reacted against the number illusion and even said that his nation would be far more advanced if the population were about half as large. It is also certain that he was the driving force behind the policy development on the population issue that has taken place in India. Moreover, he appreciated the enormous difficulties of spreading birth control among the masses as long as their levels of living were so low, but he felt that nothing really effective could be done until these levels were raised substantially."

Nehru was in favour of family planning. But Mahatma Gandhi was opposed to any artificial measures for birth control. Gandhi had faith only in self-control or abstinence. The legislative party in the Bombay Assembly was committed to the Gandhian philosophy, hence they opposed the resolution regarding measures for birth control, which was moved by Dr. Babasaheb Ambedkar. Nehru spoke clearly against Gandhi's continence or self-control.

The Planning Commission was appointed in March, 1950 and the panel of health programmes of the Commission appointed a Committee in April, 1951 to get the report on population growth and family planning to review the situation. Incorporating its key recommendations, the Draft Outline of the First Five Years Plan, which was released in July, 1951 reported that "population policy is essential to planning and family planning is a step 'toward' improvement in health, especially of mothers and children".[10] The Macro effect of family planning, that is, a lowered rate of population growth, was expected to occur only "over a period of time", but it was expected to help improve health "immediately" because "frequent and ill-spaced births undermine the health of the mother."

The Planning Commission accepted the recommendations of the Committee on population growth and family planning with respect to sterilisation as follows.[11]

1. The State should provide facilities for sterilisation or for giving advice on medical grounds.
2. Such help and advice should not be withheld from others, who seek and need it on social and economic grounds. Such

> services, however, should be provided to the extent that the personnel in hospitals and health agencies can undertake them in a manner consistent with their other duties.

In addition, State assistance and financial aid were proposed for collecting, studying and disseminating national and international information on all aspects of family limitation; for countering the ill effects of incorrect information; and for conducting research on developing inexpensive, safe, and efficacious methods of birth control suitable for all classes of people.

In recognition of some member's objection to the promotion of contraception, the Committee also proposed that non-contraceptive methods of family limitation should be investigated, along with consideration of raising the age at marriage.

The draft outline also noted that the 'increasing pressure of population' on 'inevitably limited' natural resources retards economic progress and seriously limits the rate of extension of social services, so essential to civilised existence. The complexity of the population problem, including its economic and social aspects, was recognised, but the planners held that an increase in India's labour resources would weaken, not strengthen the economy.

The final draft of the First Plan, released in December, 1952, highlighted the "urgency of the problem of family planning and population control" as a result of the decline in the death rate. It should be noted that the improvement in the standard of living required for lowering the birth rate were "not likely to materialise if there is a concurrent increase of population."

Furthermore, the plan noted, "Population control or stabilisation of the population at a level consistent with the requirements of the national economy could be achieved only through the reduction in the birth rate." But the main appeal of family planning was its potential for improving the health and welfare of the family. The Planning Commission that was bold enough to make India a pioneer in the field of population policy in 1951 was hesitant in its approach. Some of that hesitancy stemmed, of course, from that there were no precedents to follow or experiences from which to learn, but the Commission had to reckon with other factors as well such as the opposition of the Health Minister, Amrit Kaur to the use of contraceptives. Ultimately, the Prime Minister had to intervene to allow the use of contraceptives to encourage family planning.[12]

The Planning Commission created two committees—one to address policy and approach, and the other to address research and programmes on population and family planning. The main activities of these committees were to support the establishment of family planning clinics, to encourage and review ongoing research, to develop procedures for awarding grants and monitoring the grantees' progress, and to establish an institutional base.

A number of studies and pilot projects were carried out during the First Five Year Plan period to provide guidelines for the future policy and the development of a national programme. The Planning Commission allotted a sum of 65 Lakh for a family planning programme in the plan of the Ministry of Health. The Commission also considered it 'desirable': 1) to set up 'at a later date' a population commission to assess the problem; 2) to consider different views on the subject of population control; 3) to appraise the results of experimental studies; and 4) to "recommend measures in the field of family planning to be adopted by the Government and the people."

In the First Five Year Plan, emphasis was laid on the rhythm method that proved to be rather unreliable. The approach in the First Plan was research oriented and it was of exploratory nature and hence no tangible results could be obtained. The progress of the plan was reviewed by the Planning Commission. It observed that "the programme had progressed enough to call for its further development on systematic lines for continuous study of population problem and for a suitable Central Board for family planning and population problems." Thus, the Central Family Planning Board came into existence in 1956 and the post of Director of Family Planning was also created to serve in the Ministry of Health. Family Planning Boards were established in each of the several States, and Family Planning Officers were appointed for the States. So, at the beginning of the country's Second Five Year Plan, the administrative machinery, at the Centre and the States, was firmly set up to carry out the programme of family planning in India.

The population issue was dealt with at a greater length by the plan, which declared.[13] "The logic of facts is unmistakable and there is the doubt that under the conditions prevailing in countries like India, a higher rate of population growth is bound to affect adversely the rate of economic advance and living standards per capita. Given the overall shortage of land and of capital equipment relatively to population growth is an important condition for rapid improvement in incomes and in levels of living."

It is noted that the family planning programme in India has a clinical approach during the Second Plan. More and more clinics were opened so that people could take advantage of the same.

The Second Five Year Plan, 1956-61 was formulated with a limited database on population trend. Its assumptions relating to population trends allowed for a slight rise in the intercensal rate of growth from 12.5 per cent during 1950s to 13.3 per cent during the 1960s and to 14 per cent during the 1970s. Among the five specific objectives of the 'health programmes' during the Second Plan was "family planning and other supporting programmes for raising the standard of health of the people". The opening sentence of the section on family planning noted that "the problem of regulating India's population from the dual standpoint of size and quality is of the utmost importance to national welfare and national planning."

Expressing satisfaction with the progress of the family planning programme during the First Plan period, the Second Plan called for further development of the programme on 'systematic lines' for the continuous study of population problems, and for a "more or less autonomous. Central Board for family planning and population problems."[14]

Only by the end of the Second Plan period and after the publication of the Census report of 1961, it was realised that the basic assumption on which our whole planning was erected, that is to say, the rate of population growth, was largely under-estimated. The mistake was, however, corrected by the time the Third Plan was being prepared. The Third Plan proposals were considered by a special committee appointed by the Ministry of Health and by the Planning Commission's Panel on Health. Accordingly, the Third Plan also suggested that "family planning activities will be integrated with normal health services; and family services including facilities for sterilisation will be provided through medical and health centers." Family planning education was to be interwoven with other 'constructive activities', especially the work of the Primary Health Centers, community development blocks (which usually include about 1,00,000 people, and are part of a district), and voluntary organisations.

In 1963, the Report of the Director of Family Planning for 1962-63 proposed that family planning should be promoted through an extension approach. With this approach, specially trained auxiliary nurse/midwives (female health workers) were employed by the Primary Health Centers to visit married women in their homes. The health infrastructure was to be expanded substantially even though the training facility goals were to be promoted through a large band of trained workers, who would also deliver valuable assistance with health care and child-bearing to the rural population.[15] By 1963, the reorganised programme was expected to help achieve the goal of lowering the birth rate from an estimated 41-45 per 1,000 within ten years. In October, 1963 with such an optimistic projection, the Ministry of Health and Family Planning granted financial sanction for the reorganised programme, which was to be implemented in phases and would become completely functional by March, 1966.

The United Nations Advisory Mission to India recommended in 1965 a 'reinforced programme' and considered the birth rate target at 25 per 1,000 to be achievable by 1973. It emphasised the vigorous promotion of the IUD, and intensified sterilisation programme, and the promotion of the use of condoms to be distributed through commercial and other channels. To achieve these objectives, a major planning programme was initiated during 1966-67, the first year of the draft Fourth Plan.

The draft Fourth Plan, 1966-71, was prepared within the context of an estimated population growth rate of 2.4 per cent; this rate would rise further to 2.5 per cent during 1966-70. The planner recognised the family planning programme as "a key programme for the success of the country's Five Year Plans of development." The goal of the national family planning programme was a reduction in the birth rate from 40 per 1,000 populations to 25 per 1,000 'as expeditiously as possible.'

The draft Fourth Plan also proposed a marked increase in the funds allocated for the family planning programme and noted certain organisational changes. The plan also proposed: 1) recruiting a large number of female doctors for the programme; 2) involving private medical practitioners; 3) implementing the programme on a co-ordinate basis involving several ministries, including the Ministry of Information and Broadcasting, the block-level staff of the Department of Community Development, and the staff of the Ministries of Education, Local Self-Government, and Social Security, as well as various industrial organisations.

As the Fourth Plan could not start according to the original schedule, another draft was prepared for the Five-year period 1969-74.

The draft Fourth Plan, 1969-74 was based on a projection that envisaged a decline in the rate of population growth from 2.5 per cent during 1969-74 to 1.7 per cent by 1980-81 and to an average of 1.2 per cent during the subsequent 20 years. The final Fourth Plan, 1969-74, retained the thrust of the second draft, but revised the projected population estimate for the year 2000 to 890 million. The rate of population growth was expected to decline by one per cent by 2000. Population growth was seen as 'a very serious challenge' calling for "a nationwide appreciation of the urgency and gravity of the situation". The national Government had decided to keep the entire expenditure for it. The proposed plan outlay for the period 1969-74 was raised from ₹ 3.0 billion to ₹ 3.5 billion.

The draft of Fifth Plan prepared in 1974 could not be given an effective final shape. The Fifth Plan was formally approved by the National Development Council in September, 1976. It was to cover the period 1974-79, but in the wake of the 1977 elections, in which Congress Party were defeated, it was terminated prematurely in March, 1978. The draft outline of the Fifth Plan attributed the failure to attain the targeted decline in the birth rate largely to the highly ambitious targets set earlier.

The Janata Party got majority in the 1977 election and Morarji Desai, a Gandhian follower, became the Prime Minister of the country. When Dr. Babasaheb Ambedkar moved a resolution regarding measures for birth control in Bombay Assembly in 1938, at that time Morarji Desai was the Revenue Minister. He insisted on self-control instead of artificial means for birth control. After becoming Prime Minister in 1977, Morarji Desai's new Government issued a new population policy statement and reaffirmed the entirely voluntary nature of the family welfare (or family planning) programme. The Government declared itself to be "against any legislation for compulsory sterilisation either at the Central level or by the States." It also removed the use of monetary incentives to increase the acceptance of sterilisation, although it resolved to continue the pursuit of the earlier policy's other elements, including raising the age at marriage, improving female literacy, and improving the socio-economic status of women.

The number of acceptors of family planning, particularly of vasectomies, declined sharply after 1976-77. The backlash continued for at least three to four years after the emergency had been lifted and the new Government had reiterated the non coercive nature of the programme.

The Planning Commission that drafted the Sixth Five Year Plan for the period 1978-83 set up a Working Group of Population Policy. Its illustrative population projections, prepared under various assumptions about the rise in age at marriage and alternative assumptions about the level and method-mix of contraceptive use, became the basis for population goals included in the subsequent plans as well as the National Health Policy of 1983.

The goals proposed by the working group were incorporated into the final version of the Sixth Plan, 1981-85, drafted by a Planning Commission set up by Mrs. Indira Gandhi, who had returned to power in the 1980 elections. The accentuation of environmental, natural resource, and infrastructure problems as a result of the continuing high rate of population growth was noted in the Sixth Plan. The targets for sterilisation were increased to curb population growth as early and as quickly as possible. Instead of only annual targets for the users of various contraceptive methods. long-term targets were specified for the NRR (Neo Reproduction Rate) and the effective couple protection rate.

The long-term targets for the year 2000 were incorporated in the National Health Policy approved by the Parliament in 1983. The health policy is a more comprehensive document with appropriate references to the issues of maternal and child health, nutrition, and so forth. The actual performance with respect to the promotion of the family programme has fallen short of the ambitious goals set during the Sixth Pan period and subsequently.[16]

The Seventh Five Year Plan, 1985-90, continued the tradition of optimistic population projections and envisaged a decline in the rate of growth to 1.53 per cent during 1996-2001. The NRR of 1, however, was not considered likely to be reached until 2006-11. The plan envisaged better programme management, greater emphasis on MCH to reduce infant and child mortality; and a programme of health care for women, newborns and young children.

The results of the 1991 Census showed only a small decline in the average annual population growth rate during the 1980s compared with the growth rate during the preceding two decades (2.1 versus 2.2%). This nominal decline has often been interpreted as an indication that the family planning programme failed to achieve its main objective. However, the growth rate represents the deference between the birth and the death rates and is not really a good indicator of the impact of the family planning programme.

The Eight Five year plan, 1992-97, records the fears about the likely aggravation of social tensions and other problems as a result of the continuing high rate of population growth. In 1992, with the decline in the birth rate being slower than projected, the members of the Planning Commission for the Eighth Plan had to rethink their goals, and they eventually reconciled themselves to a target period of 2011-16 for reaching an NRR of 1. In the wake of recent evidence of an accelerated fertility decline, there has been an increased willingness to adopt realistic goals and to avoid overly optimistic projections.

The Technical Group, appointed by the Planning Commission, prepared population projections for the Ninth Five Year Plan, 1997-2002. It avoided the concept of the NRR of 1. Its projections were based, instead, on the fertility and mortality data gathered by the Sample Registration System, focused on the replacement level of fertility. Its extrapolation of the recent trend in the pace of declining fertility observed during the 1980s and early 1990s indicated that replacement level fertility is not likely to be achieved in the country as a whole until 2021 and, in some States, not until much later.

The Tenth Five Year Plan 2002-2007, is going on. Reduction in fertility, mortality and population growth rates are the major objectives of the Tenth Plan.[17] These will be achieved through meeting all the needs felt for improving health care of women and children. The focus has been given on improving access to services to meet the health care needs of women and children.

During the Tenth Five Year Plan (2002-2007), the main approach of the family welfare programme is:

1. To assess the needs for Reproductive and Child Health (RCH).
2. To provide need based, client centered and demand driven RCH care.
3. To strengthen the infrastructure for service delivery and bridging the gap in essential infrastructure and manpower.
4. To provide additional assistance to poorly performing districts identified on the basis of the 1991 Census and RCH surveys and ensuring uninterrupted supply of essential drugs and contraceptives.
5. To promote male participation in planned parenthood.

India's Five Year Plans reveal that the country realised the implications of rapid population growth from the very beginning.

Initially, more thrust was made on population control measures, but later the significance of child and mother health was recognised. When Planning Commission realised that family planning programme failed to achieve its main objective at that time, the Government realised the dangers of the population growth.

National Population Policy, 2000

The Karunakaran Committee of the National Development Council (NDC) proposed the formulation of a National Policy after the 1991 Census. In August, 1993, an expert group headed by Dr. M.S. Swaminathan was asked to prepare a draft of a National Policy that would be discussed by the Cabinet and then by the Parliament. The draft submitted in May, 1994 was subsequently circulated among the Members of Parliament and various agencies were asked to comment. After six years, the Government adopted it for achieving population stabilisation in the country.

The National Population Policy 2000 affirms the commitment of the Government towards voluntary and informed choice and consent of citizens while availing of reproductive health care services and continuation of the target free approach in administering family planning services.[18] The National Population Policy 2000 provides a policy framework for advancing goals and prioritising strategies during the next decade to meet the reproductive and child health needs of the people of India, and to achieve net replacement level, i.e., Total Fertility Rate (TFR) of 2.1 by 2010. It is based upon the need to simultaneously address issues of child survival, maternal health and contraception, while increasing outreach and coverage of a comprehensive package of reproductive and child health services with the Government, industry and the voluntary non-government sector, working in partnership.

The immediate objective of the National Population Policy 2000 is to address the unmet needs of contraception, health infrastructure, health personnel and to provide integrated service delivery, and bring the Total Fertility Rate to replacement level by 2010 through implementation of inter-sectoral operational strategies. The long-term objective is to achieve population stabilisation by 2045 at a level consistent with the requirements of sustainable economic growth, social development and environment protection.

The National Population Policy 2000 envisages constitution of the following bodies:

1. National Commission on Population
2. State/UT Commission on Population

The National Commission on Population was constituted on 11 May 2000 under the Chairmanship of the Prime Minister to oversee and review the implementation of the policy. The proposal of the Department of Family Welfare to reconstitute the NCP and to relocate it in the Ministry of Health and Family Welfare from the Planning Commission has been approved by the Government. The reconstituted NCP would be a compact body with 30-35 members under the Chairmanship of the Prime Minister. The reconstitution of NCP is under process.

State Population Commissions have been constituted in 17 States/UTs, viz. Andhra Pradesh, Arunachal Pradesh, Assam, Haryana, Himachal Pradesh, Jammu and Kashmir, Madhya Pradesh, Maharashtra, Meghalaya, Mizoram, Punjab, Rajasthan, Sikkim, Tamil Nadu, Andaman and Nicobar Island and Lakshadweep.

Seven State Governments have formulated their own State Population Policies with specific strategies, goals and programmes. These States are Andhra Pradesh (1997), Rajasthan (December 1999), Madhya Pradesh (January 2000), Uttar Pradesh (July 2000), Mizoram, Tripura and Gujarat (April 2002). All other States have been requested to formulate State Population Policies and constitute their respective State Population Commission. Some States are offering incentives and disincentives for the promotion of two-child norm, as a measure for achieving population stabilisation. The Government of India does not support such measures, which are in violation of the National Population Policy, 2000 and has advised the States to review these initiatives so that they are in consonance with the letter and spirit of the National Population Policy, 2000. A National Level Resource Committee has also been constituted to guide the States in the formulation of the State Population Policy.

The National Population Policy has listed short and long term goals to be achieved for population stabilisation and achievement of key Socio-Demographic indicators by the year 2010 to 2045. One of the key objectives is attainment of Total Fertility Rate (TFR) of 2.1 by 2010 for the country. It is felt that although progress in some States is satisfactory, poor performance in Bihar, Uttar Pradesh, Madhya Pradesh, Rajasthan and Orissa is proving to be a drag on national achievement. Therefore, unless urgent and focused interventions are undertaken to address the issues of reproductive and child health care in these States, the attainment of the demographic goal set in the NPP, 2000 seems unlikely. The three new States of Uttaranchal, Jharkhand and Chhattisgarh have been included in the Empowered Action Group (EAG), both on account of unsatisfactory socio-demographic indicators and also to provide an impetus to the strengthening of the primary health care infrastructure, a prerequisite for efficient delivery of Family Welfare Services.

The National Population Policy had envisaged the creation of a Technology Mission to assist demographically low performing States in accelerating the pace of implementation of family welfare programmes. The Population Commission announced the creation of Empowered Action Group in the Ministry of Health and Family Welfare for undertaking measures for population stabilisation and intersectional convergence.

The Empowered Action Group constituted by order dated 20 March 2001 is an administrative mechanism that was established for the purpose of closely monitoring the implementation of Family Welfare Programmes in the EAG States to facilitate the preparation of area specific programmes to address unmet needs. The EAG is chaired by the Union Minister for Health and Family Welfare and consists of secretaries of various related Departments, Advisor, Planning Commission, NGOs and experts. Initially, eight States of Uttar Pradesh, Madhya Pradesh, Bihar, Rajasthan, Orissa, Uttaranchal, Chhattisgarh and Jharkhand have been identified as EAG States. Four business sessions have been convened so far on 18 June 2001, 13 December 2001, 29 August 2002 and 17 November 2003 respectively. During the Tenth Plan, an amount of ₹ 250 crores has been allotted under the domestic budget for EAG Schemes.

The EAG is a high powered one window clearance mechanism for approving schemes, to finalise strategies and address the gaps in the ongoing programmes, and also to facilitate intersectional convergence. It provides a specific focus on the concerned States and helps them to plan, implement and monitor interventions aimed at raising performance indicators so that they can attain the goals set for the Tenth Five Year Plan, and in the National Population Policy, 2000. The EAG functions as an over-arching mechanism, which shall oversee implementation of schemes and utilisation of funds provided under the Domestic Budget of the Department of Family Welfare and Externally Aided Projects in respect of EAG States. The EAG is competent to sanction funds for initiatives, which would have ordinarily required detailed clearances from Expenditure Finance Committee/Standing Finance Committee. The EAG is assisted by an Inter-Ministerial Sub Committee under the Chairmanship of Secretary (FW), which examines the proposals received from State Governments and cognate Departments for funding under the EAG Mechanism. The recommendations of the Sub Committee are placed before the Empowered Action Group. So far, EAG has sanctioned funds amounting to ₹ 108 crore to the eight States, to address their unmet needs in respect of RCH Camps, Outreach Camps, strengthening the rural health infrastructure including training institute, up gradation of two CHCS per district for 24 hours service, strengthening of cold chain, Public-Private partnership pilots and funding to NGOs.

The National Population Policy, 2000 has identified meeting the unmet needs for contraception, health care infrastructure and health personnel and to provide integrated service delivery as the immediate objective with the following interventions:

(i) Strengthen, community health centers, primary health centers and sub-centers.
(ii) Strengthen skills of health personnel and health service providers.
(iii) Explore the possibility of accrediting the private practitioners for a year at a time and assign to each a satellite population, not exceeding 5000 population, for whom they provide reproductive and child health services.
(iv) Review the earlier system of the licensed medical practitioners who, after appropriate certificate from the Indian Medical Association, may participate in the provision of clinical services.
(v) Involve the non-medical fraternity in counseling and advocacy so as to demystify the National Family Welfare efforts.

National Population Policy, 2000 is very important with regard to check rapid population growth. It is good in nature. But implementation is also necessary. Today, we have good National Policy, but implementation plays a major role to achieve goals of population stabilisation and achievement of key socio-demographic indicators by the year 2010 and 2045. Therefore, implementation must be followed strictly.

Relevance of Dr. Ambedkar's Views on Birth-Control

Dr. Babasaheb Ambedkar expressed his views on birth control in the manifesto of Independent Labour Party in 1936. After that, he moved resolution about birth control and expressed his views through the speeches. But, nobody could understand his views regarding birth control. After the independence, Indian planners realised that rapid growth of population size would thwart the economic development of the country. In 1951, India became the first country in the developing world to initiate a State-sponsored family planning programme. The Indian government saw the programme not only as a way to lower the country's fertility level and population growth rate, but also as part of a broader economic and social development plan. Though in 1938, the Indian Leaders could not understand Dr. Ambedkar's views, but after independence, they realized the problem of population growth and how the rapid population growth is becoming an obstacle in the economic and social development of the country.

After fifty years of family planning programme, India's population is increasing day by day. Growth of population is becoming very serious problem in the country. That is why Indian Government has adopted the National Population Policy in February, 2000, which provides for adopting a holistic approach for achieving population stabilisation by 2045. It means that India is facing rapid population growth. Hence, India needs policies of birth-control to avoid rapid population growth. Government has expended thousand crore rupees on family planning programmes. Table 5.1 shows the expenditure of Government on family planning programme.

Family planning programmes were allotted 26,126 crore rupees in the Tenth Five Year Plan. It means that large amount is being spent for the family planning programmes. It is clear that the Government is giving importance to family planning. Had Indian leaders understood the views of Dr. Ambedkar regarding birth control, we could have been able to stabilise the Indian population. Now, the National Population Policy, 2000 envisages that India should achieve a stable population by the year 2045.

Table 5.1: Expenditure on Family Planning Programme

Period Years	*Years*	*Outlay (Rs. in Crores)*
First Plan	1951-1956	0.65
Second Plan	1956-1961	5.00
Third Plan	1961-1966	27.00
Annual Plans	1966-1969	82.90
Fourth Plan	1969-1974	285.80
Fifth Plan	1974-1978	285.60
Annual Plans	1978-1980	228.00
Sixth Plan	1980-1985	1309.00
Seventh Plan	1985-1990	2868.00
Annual Plans	1990-1992	1424.00
Eighth Plan	1992-1997	6195.00
Ninth Plan	1997-2002	14968.70
Tenth Plan	2002-2003	4930.00
Annual Plan	2003-2004	4930.00
Annual Plan	2004-2005	5500.00

Western countries have been warning us about the population bomb, which is the rhetorical summing up of the dangers inherent in explosive population growth in developing countries of Asia and Latin America. Dr. Ambedkar gave us warning about population explosion 67 years ago. He had given the reference of great sexologist Havelock Ellis. Dr. Ambedkar quoted Havelock Ellis' opinion, "Sterilisation is the best and safest method of birth-control. There can be no doubt that it will eventually be so regarded."[19] And he suggested that sterilisation is the only solution to reduce the increasing population.

T.S. Jadhav, MLA, while opposing to the resolution said, "It is a pity that honourable members should try to import Western ideas and methods into our country." Then he said, "I do not think artificial birth-control is the only method for controlling population."[20]

Jadhav advocated that self-control is the best remedy for birth-control. The measures recommended by Mahatma Gandhi should be adopted, i.e., self-control.[21]

Now time has shown that Mr. Jadhav's thought is not relevant. Dr. Ambedkar's views were relevant at that time and now also. India has adopted sterilisation as the best method of birth-control, which was suggested by Dr. Ambedkar.

The Government of India has formulated National Population Policy for birth-control. All these things indicate that Dr. Ambedkar's views regarding population growth are relevant today also. Though, then, the Bombay Government had not accepted measures regarding birth-control, but now not only Maharashtra Government, but also all the State Governments and Central Government have accepted all the measures for birth-control, which were suggested by Dr. Ambedkar.

Dr. Babasaheb Ambedkar's thought was in the right direction, which was also in the interest of the nation. He aptly said that rapid population growth is harmful to people and the nation. He has also clearly explained that pressure of population creates social and economic problems. Unfortunately, he was criticised for his right thinking. Now time has proved that Dr. Ambedkar's perspective was right. All of his views are in national interest, for the welfare of the mankind and the protection of the interests of the nation. Nobel laureate and eminent economist, Dr. Amartya Sen had explained that growth of population was harmful for poverty. Same thing was explained by Dr. Ambedkar in his manifesto of the Independent Labour Party in 1936. Hence, he moved the resolution regarding measures for birth-control. But due to the impact of Gandhian philosophy, all his efforts went in vain. After many years, time has proved that Dr. Ambedkar's views are relevant. India cannot attain social and economic development unless the rapid birth rate is controlled. This study proves that Dr. Ambedkar's views regarding birth-control were relevant in those days. But they are more relevant today than ever before.

REFERENCES

1. Conference of State Population Commissions/Councils Proceeding and An overview of the Demographic Scenario in India, National Commission on Population, Delhi, p. 29.
2. *Ibid*, p. 29.
3. *The Indian Express*, Nagpur, 19 November 2005.
4. *The Hitwada*, Nagpur 19 September 2005.
5. Salkar, K.R. (1989), *Population Education for Developing Countries*, Sterling Publishers Pvt. Ltd., Delhi, p. 68.
6. Sinha, P.N. *Population Education and Family Planning*, p. 37, 38.
7. *Ibid*, p. 38.
8. Myrdal, Gunner Quoted by Hans Raj in his book, *Population Studies*, Surjeet Publications, 1993, p. 101.
9. Gunner, Myrdal (1967), *Asian Drama*, Vol. II, Pantheon, New York.
10. Sinha, P.N., *op. cit.*, p. 40.

11. *Ibid*, p. 40.
12. *Ibid*, p. 41.
13. Second Five Year Plan, Planning Commission, Delhi, 1956.
14. Sinha, P.N. *op. cit.*, p. 42.
15. *Ibid*, p. 46.
16. *Ibid*, p. 59.
17. Annual Report 2004-2005, Ministry of Health and Family Welfare, Government of India, p. 166.
18. *Ibid*, p. 165.
19. Bombay Assembly Debates, Vol. 4, Part 57, p. 4097.
20. *Ibid*, p. 4038.
21. *Ibid*, p. 4038.

6

Summary and Conclusion

Dr. Babasaheb Ambedkar extensively contributed to various economic issues covering concrete economic problems of the country. Further, what is creditable is that most of his writings related to the pre-independence period reflect not only unique freshness in terms of his ideas, but also his deep insights into the problems. He approached and examined the economic issues with such foresight that his analysis and treatment of some of them is very much relevant even today.

Dr. Babasaheb Ambedkar founded the Independent Labour Party as a political party in 1936. He referred to the problem of over-population in the election manifesto of his Independent Labour Party and said that over-population was the major cause of poverty in India. He moved the resolution regarding the measures for birth control in the Bombay Legislative Assembly on 10 November 1938. He was probably the only political leader in India, who had strongly advocated the measures for birth control. Gandhi opposed any artificial measures for birth control. Gandhi had faith only in the concepts of self-control or abstinence. The ruling Congress Party was committed to Gandhian philosophy and, therefore, members of the Congress Party in the Bombay Assembly were against the measures for birth control. When the resolution was put to voting, 11 members, who were mainly from the Independent Labour Party, supported the move and all other 52 members opposed it. Thus, the resolution moved by Dr. Babasaheb Ambedkar could not be passed.

Since 1950, there has been tremendous increase in population in most of the developing countries, which was unprecedented and could not be anticipated earlier. In 1930, the world population was only two billion. It became three billion after 30 years in 1960. The world population in 2000 was recorded as six billion. It means that the world population has increased approximately three billion during 1960-2000, in a period of forty years. Therefore, there is a serious problem of population explosion in the world.

India's population was 25.12 crores in 1921. According to the 2001 Census, the population of India was 102.70 crores. India's population is increasing rapidly since 1931. In the last 50 years since 1951, the population of the country has increased from 36.11 crores to 102.70 crores. The average annual exponential growth rate between 1991 and 2001 is 1.93 per cent. The birth rate in India is very high. It was 25.4 in 2001, but the death rate was only 8.4. High birth rate is a special feature of undeveloped countries. Many economic and non-economic factors are responsible for this high birth rate. The death rate was 27.4 in 1950. But, it decreased and the death rate during 1991-2001 was 8.9. Presently, India has 16.87 per cent of the total world population. Rapid increase in population is very harmful for the country.

It is obvious that India has a serious problem of over population. Had Indians understood the vision of Dr. Babasaheb Ambedkar regarding the population problem, there would not have been any population problem in India.

Population Theories

Since very initial stages in the development of demographic studies of the society, demographers have developed various population theories to explain the rise in world population and its advantages as well as its disadvantages. Confucius and other Chinese thinkers, at the very initial stage of development, realised that population explosion could dislocate the economic system of a nation. Both Plato and Aristotle considered the question of optimum size of population in their discussions of the ideal type of a City-State. Medieval Christian writers considered questions of population almost entirely from a moral and ethical standpoint.

The prevailing tendency, however, was to favour population increase, as it had been in earlier times. The high rates of mortality, which was prevalent throughout the world, and the constant threat of sudden depopulation through famines, epidemics and wars predisposed ancient and medieval writers alike to favour the maintenance of a high birth rate.

The economic interpretation of the population size started only in the fourteen century. Ibn Khaldun expounded in detail a theory of cyclical variation of population and their relation to economic, political and socio-psychological conditions. Botero, an Italian of the sixteenth century, set forth ably some of the arguments later developed by Malthus.

Biologists, Sociologists, Economists and other thinkers have given their own views about population growth and the problems associated with it. Sociologist and economist have tried to attribute growth and explosion of population to social and economic causes.

Malthusian Theory

One of the earliest attempts to explore the demographic-economic relationship in an explicit manner was Malthus' theory of population. Malthus believed in the dictum that man's ability to reproduce was greater than his ability to produce. This was the central idea of his population theory. According to Malthus, food is necessary to the life of man and, therefore, exercises a strong check on population. Human population increases faster than food production. Whereas population increases in geometric progression, food production increases in arithmetic progression. Population always increases when the means of subsistence increases, unless prevented by some powerful and obvious checks. There are two types of checks, which keep population on the same level as the means of subsistence. They are preventive and positive checks.

Malthus's theory has been criticised on various accounts. In fact, his theory raised a big controversy not only during his own times, but it still remains open to criticism. Though Malthus has been much criticised for his theory, yet it is wrong to think that his thoughts on population were without any basis. His basic principle that population growth should be checked is today very much championed by the propagators of family planning progarmme.

Neo-Malthusian Theory

Recently Neo-Malthusian theory has come to the front. These thinkers have faith that whatsoever Malthus said about population growth was absolutely correct. New-Malthusians believed that without any effect on the sexual pleasure of the couple, the growth of population should be checked. This should be done with the help of recent devices and methods.

Modern economists have rejected the Malthusian theory of maximum population, which, if exceeded, will spell misery in the country. Instead of maximum population, the modern economists have substituted the idea of the optimum population.

The Theory of Optimum Population

Optimum population means the ideal number of the population that a country should have, considering its resources. The optimum means the best and the most desirable size of a country's population. It is the right number. When a country's population is neither too big nor too small, but just that much, which the country ought to have, it is called the optimum population.

Though different scholars have tried to define optimum population in their own way, yet all agree that optimum population of a country is that, which helps in maximum production with the help of other natural resources of the country. In other words, it is a point at which the per capita income is the maximum and the production is the minimum.

Though the theory of optimum population is definitely an improvement on the theory expounded by Malthus, yet the critics have pointed out certain important defects of the theory.

Theory of Demographic Transition

The process of economic development, which has transformed agrarian economies into urban, industrialised and market-oriented economies, has led to the emergence of a new theory, viz., the theory of demographic transition. The course of population growth since Malthus has been different from what he predicted. This course is more correctly described by this new theory. The theory of demographic transition brings out the relation between population growth and economic development.

Dr. Babasaheb Ambedkar's Views on Birth-Control

In the aims and objectives of Independent Labour Party, Dr. Babasaheb Ambedkar mentioned programmes regarding economic, social reform, rural reconstruction, education and administration. He suggested twelve point programme to solve the economic problems. The title of the twelve point programmes was "Pressure of Population". In the election manifesto of Independent Labour Party, he mentioned that the real causes of poverty among the farmers were due to the division of farming lands and growing population.

Dr. Ambedkar was a strong supporter of birth-control. Therefore, he moved resolution regarding measures for birth-control. He suggested measures for birth control, which, according to him, were the only remedy to arrest the rising population.

Dr. Ambedkar argued that birth-control is the only sovereign solution that can do away with all calamities. Whenever a woman is disinclined to bear a child for any reason whatsoever, she must be in a position to prevent conception and bringing forth progeny should be entirely dependent on the choice of women. Society would in no way profit by the addition of unwanted progeny. Only those children, who are welcomed by their parents, can be of social benefit and, hence, every woman must be able to resort to the prevention of conception quite easily.

Dr. Ambedkar pointed out that poverty was the root cause of immorality and birth-control is the 'sine qua non' for every progress, so one must consider the means to attain that end. He was in favour of contraception. Contraception is an important measure of birth-control. Therefore, he gave examples of western countries. Through these examples of western countries, he stated that modern contraception is utilised by people of all races, religions and strata.

Dr. Ambedkar argued that it is, therefore, obvious that all those, who stood for permanent universal brotherhood, must discontinue every attempt at increase of number and must try their best to limit populations by means of birth control.

Dr. Ambedkar held that the main object of the movement for birth-control is to bring about a state of things wherein every country will have its birth-rate suitably reduced so that it would, thus, be able to maintain its population decently with the aid of its own produce. He appealed to the members of the Bombay Legislative Assembly that birth-control movement had afforded such an opportunity to the Provincial Government and it was hoped that they would not let it slip, but would fully utilise it to their and people's benefit.

Unfortunately, members of the Bombay Legislative Assembly opposed the resolution moved by Dr. Ambedkar. Many members criticised Dr. Ambedkar for his measures on birth-control. Though the resolution was negative in the Assembly, however, he did not give up that subject. While delivering speech before the students, he convinced the students why there must be limited family. He advised the students not to produce more children. If they produce more children, then it would be very difficult to carry the burden of their food and education. He believed that small family was the key to happiness. Parents can give good education and better upbringing to their children only in small families.

Impact of Population Growth on Economic and Social Development

Rapidly growing population is a main problem in developing countries of Asia, Africa and Latin America. Rapid population increase poses a serious threat to the development efforts of less developed countries. Population growth has a bad impact on economic and social development of the nation. That is why population growth is the main obstacle in the economic and social development of the developing countries.

Impact of Population Growth on Economic Development

The economic development of a country is closely related to the qualitative as well as quantitative structure of its population. Population growth can be both stimulant as well as an obstacle to economic development. Though some economists and writers explain that population growth is a stimulant to economic development. But, it is only one side of the population growth. Many empirical studies on population have revealed that population growth does not work as a stimulant to economic development, but it is an obstacle to economic development. Following are the adverse impact of population growth on economic development.

1. *Impact on Per-Capita Income*: The per-capita income of a country has a direct relationship with its population size. If population is constant, per capita income will increase, but if the population is increasing, then, per-capita income will decrease. Hence, faster growth rate of population affects adversely the per capita income. Every increase in population decreases the per-capita national income.

2. *Impact on Capital Formation*: Rapidly growing population is a hurdle in the way of capital formation. A high rate of capital formation is very important for the development of any country. But the fast growing population makes it difficult to achieve this objective. This is done in two ways: i) It eats away investment resources and ii) It leads to lower savings.
3. *Impact on Land Resource*: The land of the nation and its underground resources do not increase, therefore, as the population increases, the proportion of per capita land decreases. Density of population is very high in India. It was 117 in 1951. But, due to rapidly increasing population, the density has increased to 324 per sq. km in 2001.
4. Impact on Natural Capital: Natural capital of a nation means the natural resources of that nation, which get affected adversely with over-growth of population and improper exploitation of these resources. Large population does much harm to the capital given to us by nature.
5. *Impact on Food Supply*: Malthus explained about the problem of population versus food supply. According to the Planning Commission of India, the main reason of our food problem is the growth rate of population, which is greater than the food production.
6. *Impact on Consumers*: Population can be broadly divided into productive consumers and unproductive consumers. Productive consumers mean labour force of the country. Unproductive consumers comprise persons, who are not engaged in employment. Population growth adversely affects productive consumers.
7. *Impact on Employment*: An overpopulated country has to face the serious problem of unemployment and under-employment. The increasing population creates the burning problem of unemployment. No country can solve the problem of unemployment without reducing the population growth.
8. *Impact on Poverty*: People do not get employment due to increasing population. Food production is not increasing with the rate of population growth. Thus, eventually, the growth of population influences poverty.
9. *Impact on Technical Advancement*: Population growth also influences technical advancement and, in fact, the whole process of gaining and importing technical know-how. Thus,

it is clear that increasing population is a great obstacle in the economic development of developing countries like India.

Impact of Population Growth on Social Development: Like economic development, there is also adverse impact of population growth on social development. A country cannot achieve social development due to increasing population. Many empirical studies observed that over-populated countries have less social development.

Following are the adverse impact of the increasing population on social development.

1. *Poverty*: Rapid increasing population is the main cause of poverty. Poverty is a social phenomenon in which a section of the society is unable to fulfill even the basic necessities of life.
2. *Quality of Life*: Quality of life means when survival is the most pressing problem before us. The rapid rising population of our country without concomitant socio-economic development is a serious threat to our survival.
3. *Urbanisation*: Population growth is the important factor of urbanisation. The rising trend leads towards urbanisation, as a result there is a huge rise in urban population, and concentration of the major proportion of urban population is in larger cities.
4. *Housing*: The problem of housing is created due to increasing population. In India, the urban housing shortage is very tragic. So far, the Government has not achieved the target in providing adequate housing facilities to growing population.
5. *High Infant Mortality Rate*: Increasing population has an impact on the infant mortality rate. Developing countries have high infant mortality rate due to over-population.
6. *Education*: Impact of population growth on education is very adverse. It is the need of time to keep strict control on the population growth.
7. *Natural Recreation Areas*: Rapid population growth has outstripped the carrying capacity of local resources, so the protected areas become especially vulnerable.

It is clear that rapid increasing population becomes a hurdle in economic and social development. Hence, it is the need of age to control the birth rate.

Dr. Ambedkar's Views—Their Relevance in Modern Age

The most important problem India is facing is the size and growth of its population. In 2001, the population of India was 102 crore, 87 lakh, 37 thousand, and 436. India accounts for a meager 2.4 per cent of the world surface area of 135.79 million sq. km. Yet it supports and sustains a whopping 16.7 per cent of the total world population. In the 50 years since 1951, the population of the country has increased from 36.11 crores to 102.87 crores. The average annual exponential growth rate between 1991 to 2001 is recorded at 1.93 per cent. The net addition to our population during the last decade was about 181 million. On this basis, the population of India is likely to reach about 119.70 crores by 2011. Beyond this period, the population projections vary depending upon the assumptions made about fertility and mortality rates. However, it is felt that India's population will reach about 140 crores by the year 2026.

Thus, in the twenty five years after 2001, we are going to add about 37.3 crore more people in our population, which is about 133 per cent of current population of the USA and 176 per cent of the present population of Indonesia—the countries next to China and India in population size now. Indian population is still growing very fast; the pressure of numbers on the natural resources of the country is beyond the limit to grow. The population explosion will continue to remain the single major hindrance in the path of the country's progress for many more decades to come.

It is the reality of India regarding population growth. Dr. Babasaheb Ambedkar was aware of the population explosion, therefore, he warned against the alarming population growth. Unfortunately, his views went unheeded.

After getting Independence, Indian planners realised that rapid growth of population and the absolute population size would throw away the economic development of the country. The Planning Commission was appointed in March 1950 and the panel on health programmes of the commission appointed a Committee in 1951 to get the report on population growth and family planning to review the situation. The Planning Commission accepted the recommendations of the Committee on Population Growth and Family Planning with respect to sterilisation. A number of studies and pilot project were carried out during the First Five Year Plan period to provide guidelines for the future policy and development of a national programme.

India's Five Year Plans reveal that the country realised the implications of rapid population growth from the very beginning. Initially, more thrust was put on population control measures, but later, the significance of child and mother health was recognised. When Planning Commission realised that family planning programme failed to achieve its main objective at that time, the Government realised the dangers of population growth.

Indian Government adopted the National Population Policy in February 2000, which provides for a holistic approach for achieving population stabilisation in the country. The National Population Policy 2000 provides a policy framework for advancing goals and prioritising strategies during the next decade, to meet the reproductive and child health needs of the people of India, and to achieve net replacement level, i.e., Total Fertility Rate (TFR) of 2.1 by 2010. The long term objective is to achieve population stabilisation by 2045, at a level consistent with the requirements of sustainable economic growth, social development and environment protection. It is clear that the Government is giving importance to birth control and family planning.

These programmes indicate that Dr. Babasaheb Ambedkar's view regarding birth control are correct. After many years, time has proved that Dr. Ambedkar's view are relevant today also. India cannot do social and economic development unless the rapid birth rate is controlled. This study proves that Dr. Ambedkar's views regarding birth-control were relevant in those days; and they are more relevant today than ever before.

Conclusion

After the detailed study of Dr. Babasaheb Ambedkar's views on birth-control and its relevance in modern India, the researcher has drawn conclusions from the study, which are mentioned below:

1. This study has proved that high growth rate of population affects the social, economic and educational progress of the country. Hence, rapid growing population is the main problem in developing countries of Asia, Africa and Latin America. Many social, economic and other problems are created due to increasing population.
2. India is an over-populated country. It has high birth rate compared to developed countries. India's population is

growing rapidly since 1931. In 2001, the population of India was 102.87 crores, which is 16.7 per cent of the world population. India's population will reach about 140 crores by the year 2026. It means that India is facing the problem of population explosion, which is very serious for the country and its development.

3. Dr. Babasaheb Ambedkar strongly advocated birth control. He had given more importance to the measures for birth control. He moved the resolution regarding measures for birth control. However, other people were against the measures, which were suggested by him. Hence, the Government could not take the problem of increasing population seriously. That is why there wasn't a check on the population growth before 1950.
4. After the independence, the Planning Commission realised the problem of population growth. Then, the Government of India gave importance to the family planning programmes. However, family planning programme could not achieve its target due to many reasons.
5. Government of India adopted the National Population Policy in 2000. The policy enumerates certain socio-demographic goals to be achieved by 2010. The long-term objective is to achieve population stabilisation by 2045. Nowadays, the Government has realised the problems associated with the explosion of population.
6. Dr. Babasaheb Ambedkar had suggested that measures of birth control were the only remedy to check the population growth. After many years, time has proved that Dr. Ambedkar's views are relevant in the modern age.
7. World Bank Survey, UNESCO and empirical studies have observed that increasing population is the hurdle in the way of development. Dr. Ambedkar had also advocated that without a check on population, the country could not develop.

In short, the attempts are made to prove that Dr. Babasaheb Ambedkar's views regarding birth-control were not only relevant in those days, when having a tremendous foresight, Dr. Ambedkar advocated for it, but they are relevant even today.

Appendix

*On Measures for Birth-Control**

Mr. P.J. *Roham (Ahmednagar South):* Sir, I beg to move—

> "This Assembly recommends to Government that in view of the urgent need of limiting the family units, Government should carry on an intensive propaganda in favour of birth-control among the masses of this Province and should provide adequate facilities for the practice of bith-control." Question proposed.

Mr. P.J. *Roham (Addressed the House in Marathi):* The educated class has, by this time, fully realized the necessity of birth-control and fortunately the leaders in our country also are unanimous on this point Pandit Jawaharlal Nehru, Sir Ravindranath Tagore and Mrs. Sarojini Naidu, know very well the importance and the urgency of the movement for birth-control and are in favour of contraceptives. Babu Subhash Chandra Bose, the President of the Indian National Congress, said in his presidential speech:

> "If the population goes up by leaps and bounds, as it has done in the recent past, our plans are likely to fall through."

Even Mahatma Gandhi has written long ago as follows: "I must not conceal from the reader the sorrow I feel when I hear of births in this land."

---

* Speech delivered by Shri P. J. Roham. He has expressly stated that the speech was based in all respects on the points drawn by Dr. Ambedkar for his own speech and that Dr. Ambedkar is the father of this speech. Shri Roham further states that he was complimented by Dr. Ambedkar for almost reproducing the speech which, he had contemplated to deliver in the Assembly on that day, i.e. on 10th November 1938.

B.L.A., *Debates* Vol. 4 (Part 3), November 1938, pp. 4024-38.

Very few have an adequate idea of the immense loss sustained by children born of persons who are handicapped either physically, mentally or financially. The parents as well as the society also suffer very much. The prevention of the births of such children would considerably reduce the death-rate among mothers who succumb to child-birth and its concomitant diseases, lower infantile mortality, improve public health by removing the many diseases due to want of even the prime necessaries of life felt by many persons, check the offences perpetrated by persons suffering from intense poverty and would bring about an all-round uplift of society by affording full scope to its spiritual advancement.

The present keen struggle of life renders timely marriage impossible for many and thus exposes them to various diseases and habits. Many women become invalid for life and some even lose their lives by the birth of children in their diseased condition or in too great numbers or in too rapid succession. Attempts at abortion, resorted to for the prevention of unwanted progeny, exact a heavy toll of female lives. Unwanted children are often neglected by their mothers and hence they become nothing but a burden to society which is further deteriorated by the addition of defective progeny from diseased persons. Birth-control is the only sovereign specific that can do away with all these calamities. Whenever a woman is disinclined to bear a child for any reason whatsoever, she must be in a position to prevent conception and bringing forth progeny which should be entirely dependent on the choice of women. Society would in no way profit by the addition of unwanted progeny. Only those children who are welcomed by their parents, can be of social benefit and hence every woman must be enabled ***to*** resort to prevention of conception quite easily.

Poverty is the root-cause of immorality. The following passage from the essay read by Prof. Dr. Tondler before the Congress at Vienna in 1933 would show the evil consequences of insufficiency of living accommodation, The professor said, "On the average every family gets one room in Germany two and a half rooms in France and three rooms in England. Seventy-five thousand families had no tenements of their own in Berlin in 1925. The result is that children sleep with the adults not only in the same room but also in the same bed. Many children lose their lives by the overcrowding in insanitary dwellings. Whole families are stricken with veneral diseases. Girls have to succumb to sexual intercourse even before they are mature. Sexual connections often take place between parents and their children and brothers and sisters. The boys learn to commit thefts and the girls become prostitutes. The same condition prevails at Vienna. In 1919, out of the tenements let out, 10 per cent, had only one small room; 37 per cent. had one big room and 23 per cent, had one small room and one big room. Out of the children between the ages of fourteen and eighteen who maintained themselves, twenty per cent, had no separate beds of their own. Towns and villages fare even worse."

In our country, the same condition prevails in cities like Bombay. A few exceptions apart, it is observed that virtue is palsied where poverty prevails Further on it will be shown how it is well-nigh impossible to uproof poverty without the aid of birth-control.

When we have thus realised that birth-control is the *sine qua-non for* every progress, we must consider the means to attain that end. To be satisfied with only that much of sexual enjoyment that is necessary for getting the desired number of children and to banish sexual thoughts from one's mind when progeny is not required, is one of the ways. The use modern contraceptives is the other way. As for the first way, it must remembered that while continence in the unmarried state may be possible, *it is* nothing but displaying ignorance about human nature to expect that young and healthy married couples, living together and fond of each other, can observe continence for years together. The cases of strong-willed persons, whose minds are not affected in the presence of objects of enjoyment, apart, there is no doubt that ordinary human beings are bound to fall a prey to the influence of enticements. Is it not strange, therefore, that this fact, which is as clear as daylight, is denied by some.

Self-control has been proved to be absolutely useless for birth-control from the experience of several countries and ages. Even the advocates of continence cannot claim that ordinary persons will be able to eschew sexual intercourse altogether throughout their lives. The laying aside of continence even for a single day every year may lead to an annual conception. Even, if we assume that self-control enables certain persons to bring about birth-control, we cannot draw the conclusion that others will be able to follow them. It is necessary to remember that just as appetite for food differs in the case of different persons, so sexual appetite also varies from person to person.

Strict observance of certain rules laid down in Hindu scriptures necessitates the neglect of the ideal of family-limitation. For instance, verse 8, Chapter 54, of "Vishnu Smriti" enjoins sexual intercourse on certain specified days.

Sir, honourable members have received a pamphlet written by Mrs. Sarojini Mehta, M.A., I am not going to read the whole pamphlet, but will quote only a few passages from it:

> "Whenever the subject of birth-control is broached, the burden of our opponents' song is that continence (Brahmacharya) is the sovereign specific for our country and that it is better to leave Westerners to be blessed by their own artificial remedies. I humbly supplicate these honourable persons to state the grounds upon which they hold this view. It is stated that our people are spiritualistic, while Westerners are materialistic. It has now become well-nigh nauseating to hear this parrot cry repeated. In what way are our people spiritualistic? Have our people renounced the world and become ascetics? Can mere repetition of certain catch-phrases like "All this is delusion." "One must abandon attachment to worldly lifeturn people into spiritualistic? Does not every one of our villages possess Shylocks ready to demand their pound of flesh from poor and innocent debtors? Are there not bankers mean enough to devour the deposits of widows? Have we not scoundrels who are debased enough to leave stranded helpless widows whom they themselves have misled? Can we claim that our society is without men who have discarded their chaste and devoted wives and taken to prostitutes? I am completely at a loss to understand how a society can be called spiritualistic, in which many are ruined by matrimonial transactions that amount to virtual sales of brides and bridegrooms, in which a person refusing to give and absenquial feast to his caste-people is out-casted, in which men are planning their second marriages while their first wives are burning on funeral pyres, in which even old fogies of sixty years can marry girls of twelve on the strength of monetary bribes and in which the treatment offered to widows is worse than that given even to the beasts. Western materialism cannot be held responsible for the rottem state of our society discribed above. On the contrary it is those who have come into contact with western materialism who are trying their best to remedy these evils, though their efforts are proving nothing but a cry in the wilderness."

Further on, in another paragraph, she says:

> "The conduct of Indraraj towards Ahilya, of Parashar Rishi towards Satyawati and of Suryadev towards Kunti would make those perpetrator liable for rigorous imprisonment in this age of Kali but that being considered to be Satya Yug, we not only connive at these delinquencies but raise books containing such descriptions to the status of 'Sacred Books' and insist that they must be prescribed as test-books in the curriculum for children. How many lessons on continence can pupils find in the Mahabharat, the Bhagwat and the Puranas? How can an age, that never knew what continence was, inspire us to observe that virtue? How is possible to consider that age to have observed continence in which the were incidents like the story of King Dushyanta, who first misled innocent and guileless girl living in fhe hermitage of a sage and the discarded her when she was pregnant? When one considers the number of children born to certain persons mentioned in very ancient narrative a doubt naturally arises in one's mind as to whether the people in those day ever dreamt what continence was. How can one believe that continence was observed in those times when one considers that Sagar begot sixty thousand sons and that there were a hundred Kowrawas, twenty-seven daughters of Daksha Prajapati and several other such instances? Continence was pa scant respect in bygone days. It can actually be seen that in these days is kept at a distance everywhere. The birth-rate of our country is not falling lower than that of any 'materialistic' country. Brahmacharya cannot be observed even where the life of a woman, already the mother of man children, is jeopardised by an additional delivery. It is neglected even in the families of paupers, dying of hunger, where the addition of even a single individual to the family would be nothing short of a calamity. Even these days of unemployment, when it is practically impossible to find outlets for sons, additional children are born even in middle class family every year or year and a half. In castes, in which the usage of down prevails, parents express much grief at the birth of a daughter, kill her the very outset or bring her up most negligently so that she may a natural death. They,

> however, never resort to continence to avoid the chances of girls being born. In spite of all these instances we go on proclaiming that continence alone is the ideal for our country! Of what earthly use is such conduct? We have to take into account the state of things actually existing before our eyes. There are no chances of making any improvement in our condition by mere talk of ideals."

Dr. K. B. Antrolikar: Sir, all that may be taken as read, because every member has received it.

Mr. P. J. Roham: Sir, I have made it clear that I am not going to read the whole of it. I request my honourable friend Dr. Antrolikar to have patience.

Mr. P. J. Roham: She continues:

> "If, therefore, they have got the country's welfare at heart, they ought to try their level best to popularise continence by founding associations for the purpose of carrying on the work systematically, just as the birth-controllers are doing to popularise contraceptives. If, however, they are either unwilling or unable to do anything in this matter, the hands of the champions of contraception will be strengthened."

As a doctor has wisely remarked, if men had to bear the pangs which women have to undergo during child-birth none of them would ever consent to bear more than a single child in his life.

It is wrong to hold that because the ideal of large families is before society up to this time nobody wishes to limit his family* Human beings, who earnestly desire to be saddled with large families, are rare. Ordinary[7] persons do want to limit their families and do not even flinch to have recourse to diabolical methods such as abortion, infanticide, etc. Such attempts are witnessed everywhere. From an account published by "The People's Tribune" in 1934 it is found that in 1933 over 24,000 dead bodies of little infants were picked up in the street of Shanghai alone and the saine state prevails throughout most of China. It is bitter and terrible poverty that makes the parents expose their infants. In the light of such instances, it is futile to hope that ordinary persons will be able to avoid progeny merely through self-control. It is, therefore, established that there is no go without recourse to modern contraceptives. To deny the necessity of those remedies is to show one's preference for abortions, infanticides, etc.

Some people think that they would be losers if the numbers in their particular race, religion, or region are lessened. They are afraid that their adversaries would thereby be enabled to gain ground over them. In the first place, it is necessary to remember in this connection that the rate of increase of a population does not necessarily dwindle down as soon as family limitation is resorted to. That rate is dependent not merely on the birth-rate but chiefly on the survival-rate. The experience of several scientists from different places has proved that the higher the birth-rate, the higher is the death-rate also and no sooner the birth goes down, the death-rate also declines. The result is that not only is the survival-rate not adversely affected but very often it even rises. Dr. Maria Stopes has found from the experience gained in "The Mothers' Clinic" that the greater the number of conceptions the higher is the rate of maternal and infantile mortality. Similar is the experience of other scientists. Dr. J. M. Munro, M.D., F.R.F.P.S., says in his book "Maternal Mortality and Morbidity":

> "The strongest argument in favour of limiting the family is that by the fourth birth the mortality-rate very nearly approaches that of the first birth, looked upon generally as the most serious and dangerous. After the fourth birth, the mortality rate steadily and markedly rises with each successive pregnancy and parturition. The same applies to still-births and neo-natal deaths."

Due to excessive child-mortality, the rate of growth of the population of countries like India is not equal to that of countries like England though the birth-rates in countries of the former type are higher than those in the latter type. The birth-rate of England is nearly half that of India. Yet we find that the population in England increased by nearly 23 per cent between 1901 and 1931, while the population in India rose by only 17 per cent in the same period. This will show that even for a rapid growth of numbers, the better way is to adopt the practice of birth-control and thus cut down infantile mortality.

It must also be remembered that for modern wars comparatively few persons are necessary. An army, well-equipped with modern materials for warfare, can route an army much greater in number than itself, if the latter one is not so well-equipped. In the former world war, countries of low birth-rates vanquished those with high birth-rates.

In the world, we can witness many societies that are small in numbers but distinguished in respect of wealth, culture etc. In our country, the Parsee community is an illustration on this point. To hanker after quantity is, therefore, not a very profitable ideal.

After this, it is worth while keeping in mind that it is principally poverty that is at the root of the animosity between different races, societies and countries. When poverty will be uprooted, the root-cause of much of such hatred will be eradicated and then nobody need be afraid of molestation from others.

The example of Western nations shows us that modern contraception is utilised by persons of all races, religions and strata. For instance, it is found that the notion that the Roman Catholics are against birth-control is unfounded. France is a Roman Catholic country and still it is notorious that the birth-rate in that country is quite low. The following ten countries had the lowest birth-rates in 1932:

Sweden	...	...	14.5
Germany	...	...	15.1
Austria	...	...	15.2
England and Wales	...	...	15.3
Norway	...	...	16.3
Australia	...	...	16.4
Switzerland	...	...	16.7
New Zealand	...	...	17.1
United States	...	...	17.3
France	...	...	17.3

Among the three lowest countries are Austria, which is entirely Catholic, and Germany, which is one-third Catholic. The following figures, the birth-rates of important cities, illustrate the very point. They are all for 1927 or 1928:

London	...	...	16.1
Cologne	...	...	16.0
Geneva	...	...	14.6
Milan	...	...	14.5
Turin	...	...	13.2
Prague	...	...	12.5
Munich	...	...	12.0
Vienna	...	...	10.6

With the exception of London, all the above towns are solidly Roman Catholic, yet they all have a lower birth-rate than London. Three of them are in Mussolini's Italy.

It will be thus seen that the fear, that other communities will neglect birth-control and will thus become stronger in numbers, is altogether a baseless one.

Speeches of statesmen, who are responsible for wars, clearly show that economic difficulties, due to pressure of population, are at the root of most of the modern wars, Bernhardt, the Kaiser, Hitler, Mussolini and Gooring have often stressed this pioint in no ambiguous words. For instance, Adolf Hitler says in his book, Mein Kampf:

> "Through the mad multiplication of the German people before the war, the question of providing the necessary daily bread came in an ever sharper manner into the foreground of all political and economic thought and action."

Further on he says:

> "Only an adequate amount of room upon this earth secures to a nation the freedom of its existence—The National Socialist movement must endeavour to do away with the disproportion between our numbers and our territory............ Ground and territory must be the object of our foreign politics." (pp. 728-35).

In his recent historic speech, delivered on the 12th of September 1938, Hitler says:

> "They expect Germany, where 140 persons are squeezed into a sauare kilometre, to keep her jews, whereas the powers with only a few persons per kilometer do not want them....."

Similarly Mussolini has said:

> "We are hungry for land, because we are prolific and intend to remain so." (From "Foreign Affairs October 1926).

> "Italy demands that her indisputable need of sun and land shall be recognised by all other nations. Should they fail to

do so. Italy will be forced to take matters into her own hand." (From "Sunday Times", November 14, 1926).

The Deputy Speaker: The honourable member has exceeded the time-limit.

Mr. B. K. Gaikwad: Sir, may I know what is the time-limit? *The Deputy Speaker:* Half-an-hour.

Mr. B. K. Gaikwad: On a point of information, Sir. The honourable member who moved the last resolution (Mr. Shrikant) spoke, I believe, for more than an hour.

The Deputy Speaker: Extension of the time is within the discretion of the Chair.

Mr. B. K. Gaikwad: Can that indulgence not be given to other resolutions?

Mr. P.J. Roham: Sir, I do not wish to take much time of the House, but I have still some more points to make and request you to kindly allow me some more minutes.

It is, therefore, obvious that all those who stand for permanent world-brotherhood, must discountenance every attempt at increase of numbers and must try their best to limit populations by means of birth-control.

The fear that birth-control propaganda will fail to filter down to the masses and the result of the movement will thus be dysgenic instead of eugenic, is also groundless. The experience gained in Western countries establishes the fact that the lower classes do take advantage of contraceptives as soon as they are made cognizant of them, the need being greater in their cases. The masses in our country, though illiterate, are intelligent enough to know in what their own interest lies and hence there is no doubt that they will fully utilise this invention also as soon as they are made aware of its existence. Vasectomy would be found to be useful in the case of such persons and hence Government and municipalities must provide facilities in this respect in their hospitals, etc.

The late principal Gole has clearly said that even villagers have many virtues and it is really they that replenish the supply of good citizens.

The opponents of this movement try to show its futility by pointing out the examples of France, Germany and Italy but they forget that we cannot follow these countries unless it is proved that their attempts at the increase of their populations are justified. In the first place, it must be kept in mind that the birth-rates of these nations are much lower than the birth-rate of our country. Our birth-rate is 35 whereas in 1936 the birth-rates of Italy, France and Germany were 22-2, 15 and 19 respectively. In 1900 the birth-rate in Germany was 35-6 but in 1933 it came down to 14-7. Italy and France also have their birth-rates much reduced since that time. In England the. birth-rate was 33-9 in 1851-55 but in 1931 it was lowered to 15-3. Our birth-rate is practically stationary for the last fifty years and hence it would be unwise for us to imitate the efforts of other countries towards raising that rate.

It is quite natural for imperialists to lament the slackening of the rate of increase of the people of their race and it is not surprising that they should raise cries like "Renew or Die". It is, however, strange to see that those cries should make even some educated persons suspicious about the benefits of birth-control. An article, "Renew or Die", by Sir Leo Chiozza Money in "The Nineteenth Century and After" for February 1938 will illustrate the point. This writer has assumed that white leadership is necessary for the good of all humanity and has raised a cry to arrest the decline in the number of the white people. Now, in the first place, many will refuse to admit that white supremacy has benefited the world and secondly few educated persons will be prepared to go to the length of maintaining that the decline in the number of white people will bring down any calamity upon humanity. Besides this, the postulates of this person are all wrong. He has taken it for granted that the birth-rate in England will gradually become lower and lower and that in the year 2,035 the population of England will be reduced to 4,400,000 (44 lacs). But the facts are that the birth-rate in England is increasing instead of going down. In 1933 it was 14-4 but in My 1938 it becomes 15-3. Similarly whereas the writer has estimated that the population of England and Wales in 1940 would be only 40,700,000, the actual figure for 1937 there was already 41,031,000 and it is increasing at the rate of 190,000 people per year. These facts will show that one must take the precaution of not being misled by such articles.

Emigration is sometimes suggested as a remedy for finding an outlet to over-population but that remedy also is not very promising. Compulsion in emigration, amounting to transportation is out of question. Very few persons have the courage and the inclination necessary for leaving one's own country, endeared to one's heart by reminiscences of childhood and the presence of relatives and friends and made agreeable by a suitable climate and other factors and to repair to a distant land in which there is the danger of the climate being found to be an unsuitable one and in which the inhabitants are different from oneself in language, customs and manners. Generally, people willing to emigrate are those who are fit to be good citizens and who are able and energetic. It is really a loss to the motherland that such people should emigrate. These persons can easily maintain themselves in their own country but ambition impels them to try to better their lot by going to distant lands. Emigration is practically useless in the case of persons who are handicapped either physically or mentally or financially and it is really these people that stand in need of help. Considered from the point of the necessary capital alone, this remedy cannot afford relief to many persons.

Besides this, it must be kept in mind that sparsely populated countries are unwilling to accommodate others because they require elbow-room for their own increasing progeny. Canada is a colony in the British Empire mainly inhabited by Englishmen but it is notorious that the Canadians refused to allow English labourers, who had gone there for seasonal work, to settle in their land. Wars are occasioned by the attempts of populous countries to force their entrance in sparse regions. An illustration on the point, which is quite recent and near to us, is afforded by Burma. The cause underlying the recent communal riots there was mainly the suspicion in the minds of the Burmans that Indian marred their material progress. Compared to over-populated countries, regions of sparse populations are very few, Japan, Italy, Germany, China, India and many other countries are over-populated. It is not possible to find adequate room for emigrants from all these lands.

One more point in this connection is also worth mentioning. Emigration cannot solve the population problem of a country permanently. Like air, expanding population has a tendency to fill up vacuum immediately, leading to the recurrence of the former condition and hence it is obvious that there is no go without birth-control.

Some think that as soon as child-marriages are given up and late marriages are introduced, the increase in population will be checked. But this belief also is an unfounded one. In the first place, years must elapse before the ages at which girls are married would be sufficiently raised in our country. The years of greatest fertility in the case of girls are those between 18 and 22. In Western countries, women marry after this period. That is, they marry when their time of greatest fertility is over. When we notice the difficulties in the enforcement of the

Sarda Act, fixing the minimum age of marriage of a girl at 14, we can easily see that it is almost useless to hope that in the near future women in our country will postpone their marriages *up* to 22 and population will be checked thereby. Mr. P.K. Wattal has drawn the following conclusions from the fertility-enquiry conducted specially in connection with the 1931 census.

(1) That girls married at ages below twenty give birth to a smaller number of children than girls married at ages above twenty.
(2) That the survival-rate of children born to mothers married at ages below twenty is much less than that of children born to mothers married at ages above twenty.

These conclusions show us that even when late marriages would come into vague generally, there is no chance of population being appreciably checked thereby. More children would live upto mature ages and hence there is a chance of an increase and not a decrease in the rate of growth of our population.

Dr. G.S. Ghurye, Ph.D., University Professor of Sociology, Bombay, says In his article, "Fertility Data of the Indian Census of 1931" in the "*Journal of the University of Bombay*" (Vol. III, May 1934):

> "If the above tentative conclusion about the co-relation between fertility and the age of woman at marriage should prove to be correct, then with the increase in woman's age at marriage which is quite essential, there would be an increase in the fertility of marriage. As it is, I believe our population is very large and our increase undesirable and to help its increase at a greater rate would be suicidal. With our efforts to raise the women's age at marriage, therefore, there must also be carried on an intensive campaign for control of birth."

It must not, moreover, be forgotten that prostitution is encouraged by people being unable to marry at proper ages and other evil consequences also follow thereby. It is, therefore, necessary to resort to birth-control if marriage at a proper age is aimed at.

The view is held that economic independence of women will lessen the growth of population but it also does not hold water. Economic independence has no power to free a person from the clutches of Eros. Few women can observe perfect continence throughout their lives and hence this remedy would be found to be fruitless. Even now, women of the lower classes are actually helping their families with their own earnings but that fact docs not seem to help family-limitation to any extent.

Some persons hold the view that though birth-control may be necessarily on medical and hygienic grounds, still it is not required for solving economic difficulties. They maintain that our country has got much scope for economic and agricultural development and efforts in these directions would raise the standard of life of our people appreciably. On close examination, however, this view also is found to be quite untenable. Want of sufficient capital and rich customers would prevent any material development of our industries. Similarly, insufficiency of fertile lands, rain-fall and manures stand in the way of any substantial increase in our agricultural production. Except in Assam, there is very little fertile land that has not yet been brought under cultivation. In Burma, there is even now sufficient suitable land awaiting cultivation and it was the figure of such land from that province that misled certain people into the belief that India has even yet sufficient fertile virgin land. In our province, 86-4 per cent, of the cultivable land has already been brought under the plough and it is doubtful whether even a fraction of the rest of the land is of any value. According to the Report of the Royal Commission on Indian Agriculture much of such land is worthless. A great portion of the agricultural land in our country has become barren through incessant cropping and want of sufficient manures.

Through the excessive growth of population, our country suffers from deficiency of forests and pasture-lands. In Canada 34.3 per cent. of cultivable land is reserved for pasturage. This proportion is 21.5 in France, 18.3 in Italy, 14.3 in Germany but in our country it is only 1.6. These figures will show to what strait our cattle is forced. Cast our glance in whatever direction we may come across mere skeletons of cattle. Though our people pride themselves upon their humanitarianism, they have, in their struggle for land, unjustly deprived the dumb creatures of much of their pasturage and brought it under tillage. Our agriculture, therefore, is suffering from insufficiency of useful cattle and organic manures like cow-dung, and hence it is very difficult to effect many appreciable improvements in it. Some persons point out the large produce per acre of rice in Japan and China and hold out the hope that there is scope for materially increasing our produce of that crop. There are grounds, however, to doubt the correctness of the figures of the production of rice in those countries. Count Karlo Sforra, former Minister for Foreign Affairs for Italy, contributed an article styled "The conflict between China and Japan" to a recent number of the? "International Conciliation," a monthly published from New York. It is stated therein that from 1900, there is an appreciable decrease in the rice production per acre in Japan. There is considerable evidence to show that figures about agriculture in Japan are not reliable. Besides this, notice also must be taken of the facts that Japan is blessed with plenty of timely and all-the-year round rainfall and abundance of manures due to her extensive forests and also with a climate ideally suited to her rice crops combination of advantages rarely witnessed anywhere else. Although it may be admitted that self-rule may effect some betterment of the lot of our masses, no lasting and appreciable improvement in the economic condition of our people can be hoped for unless the growth of our population is deliberately checked. As has been already explained, with every opportunity afforded for its expansion, population begins to grow rapidly and thus nullifies all the advantages secured through great efforts. Hence, experience has made many scientists to hold the view that unless precaution is taken to regulate population growth by means of birth-control along with effort to improve the economic condition of the people there cannot be any substantial and permanent rise in the standard of life of the masses.

The fact, that mere self-rule is powerless to effect an all-round improvement in the condition of a people, is demonstrated to the hilt by the examples of many independent nations. Although, through various reasons, including a low birth-rate, the economic condition of the inhabitants of countries like England and America is superior to that obtaining in this country—poverty prevents many of our countrymen from obtaining a nourishing food—still is far from satisfactory. Even there, many find it difficult to maintain a standard of life necessary for perfect health. According to President Roosevelt one-third of the inhabitants of America do not get sufficient nourishing food. One of the reasons for this is that even there birth-control is not practised to the extent to which it is necessary. There is plenty of fertile land per head in countries that are newly settled and hence the people there get more nourishing food than that obtained by persons in thickly populated nations. Here arc the figures of consumption per head per annum in Australia and Italy:

	Australia	Italy
Milk and its products (gals)	102	23
Meat (lbs.)	202	35
Fruit (lbs.)	104	40
Sugar (lbs.)	107	18
Wheat (lbs.)	297	351

Every article of food except wheat is consumed in far greater quantities in Australia than in Italy.

Out of the nations of the old world, countries like Holland that have their birth-rates much reduced through birth-control, are much happier than the rest.

In the Bombay Presidency, the amount of milk available per head per day is only one and a quarter "tolas According to authorities on nutrition, every individual must get on an average at least one pint of milk per day. The main object of the movement for birth-control is to bring about a state of things wherein every country will have its birth-rate suitably reduced so that it would thus be able to maintain its population decently with the aid of its own produce.

Some are under the impression that modern scientific discoveries have solved the problems of food for mankind and that it is only mal-distribution that is at the root of the present economic difficulties. Fair distribution of property would, in their opinion, bring about plenty everywhere. There is no doubt that in many places injustice prevails in the division of property and every impartial public worker must take all steps to secure justice for wronged persons in this respect. It is, however, necessary to remember that mere equal distribution will never be able to bring about a permanent and material amelioration of the condition of the masses unless growth of population is controlled by means of family-limitation. Land being the chief source of all wealth, there cannot be plenty for all unless plenty of fertile land falls to the share of each individual. Agricultural experts like Sir Damiel Hall and Prof. East have pointed out that about two and a half acres of cultivable land are needed to support one individual on the western European standard. But in all old countries, people have to maintain themselves on land much less than this. In India, there is only three quarters of an acre of cultivable land for each individual and, as has been already pointed out, according to the opinion of the Royal Commission on Agriculture, much of the uncultivated land in this country is practically useless. The view that the advent of chemical fertilisers has solved the problem of manures is also not a sound one. Artificial manures cannot be used at each and every place.

Rao Bahadur D.L. Sahastrabudhe, M.Ag. M.Sc., retired Agricultural Chemist to the Government of Bombay, wrote in his article in "Sahyadri" for October 1936 as follows:

> "Experience has shown that artificial manures cannot be utilised everywhere. Organic manures like cow-dung must accompany the use of chemical fertilisers. Otherwise, artificial manures do not prove to be congenial (o the crops. Similarly the crop that is to be manured with chemical fertilisers must have plentiful supply of water to prevent an injury to it.

Besides this, it must be noted that the two chief fertilisers are nitrates and phosphates and neither is of much use without the other. The supply of phosphates, however, is very limited. Sir Federick Keeble says:

'Nearly all the soil of the world are famishing for phosphates. (Fertilisers and Food Production) (1932), p. 221. Professor Armstrong says:

> 'The solution of the nitrogen problem by Crookes has brought us nearer to destruction rather than saved us, by hastening the depletion of irreplaceable phosphatic stores.'."

Almost all places are suffering from inadequacy of forests and as a result thereof there is also a shortage of water and manures. The present Congress Government are trying to uplift the masses of this Bombay Presidency (hear, hear). But all their efforts will go in vain if the population problem is not tackled by means of birth-control. *The Deputy Speaker:* The Honourable Member may now bring his remarks to a close. *Mr. P. J. Roham:* Yes, Sir. Dr. Radhakamal Mukerjee has in his book, "Food Planning for 400 Millions" states:

> "Unless some check is placed upon population-growth, any other! remedy fends to be only temporary, as in the latter country (China), for population will rapidly rise again to the maximum number of persons] the land will support. As population outruns faster the educational facilities that may be provided, while the taxable capacity hardly increases, it is

> clear that the pressure of population cannot be viewed merely in relation to the food-supply. An expanding population makes readjustments more and more difficult. A rational family planning and education of the masses in With-control, must be accepted as the most effective means of combating population increases."

Bombay is the gateway of India and this movement also entered this country through that very gate. It would be in the fitness of things, therefore, that it should also be nurtured in this very province. Few people get an opportunity for doing acts that would immortalize their names. Birth-control movement has afforded such an opportunity to our provincial government and it is hoped that they will not let it slip but will fully utilize it to the benefit of themselves and the people.

> *"The good things of this earth do not fall from heaven, every progress has its bill of cost and only those who pay for it, will have that progress."*
>
> *—Dr. Babasaheb Ambedkar*

Index